# Sacred Space

*Explore the Sacred Space of Five World Religions*

An Invitation to

# Explore the Sacred Space

## of

# Five World Religions

Ben Campbell Johnson, editor

ISBN-13: 978-1460975640
ISBN-10: 1460975642

Copies of this book may be ordered from:

www.Amazon.com

or

The Community Institute Press
669 East Side Ave SE
Atlanta GA 30316

# Contents

# Preface

**The idea for this book emerged naturally.** Dr. Ben Campbell Johnson, Professor Emeritus of Columbia Theological Seminary, had successfully organized and coordinated several group excursions that brought 30-50 Christians into the sacred spaces and communities of Muslims, Jews, Buddhists and Hindus. The purpose of the excursions was to give members of the majority faith opportunities to listen, observe, and engage the others in the midst of their worship and within their worship environment.

To deliver an authentic and substantive program, Dr. Johnson solicited talented collaborators from each faith to serve as planners, leaders, and hosts for the visits. Thus far, evaluations from participants have rated the Interfaith Immersions as "outstanding, eye-opening, engaging, insightful and a life-changing experience." Immersion is designed to enable people of diverse faiths to begin essential relationships as neighbors of faith with one another.

In the process of the work and the planning, the coordinating team of a Christian, Muslim, Jew, Buddhist, and Hindu became quite close and connected. It is from this work and these relationships that the idea for this book, *Explore the Sacred Space of Five World Religions*, was born.

Under the gentle and encouraging leadership of Ben Johnson, these five contributors – Mitch Cohen, Gareth Young, Tom Buchanan, Gillian Renault, and Imam Plemon T. El-Amin – have produced an insightful work that takes the reader inside the sacred spaces, the traditions, the symbols, the hearts and the wisdom of five of the world religions coexisting in Metropolitan Atlanta. They open the doors to their Church, Synagogue, Masjid, Temple, and Center, and share both the seen and the unseen. As Christian Tom Buchanan writes, "Every space tells a story. It communicates something about those who use the room... who they are...what they care about...perhaps even what they hope for." In relating some of the rituals that occur within the sacred space of the Church, Buchanan describes the Sacraments as "an outward sign of an invisible grace – a physical, tangible act that demonstrates a deeper spiritual reality."

**Imam Plemon T. El-Amin** shares with readers the love and respect Muslims have for the Masjid (Mosque) which plays such a central role in Islamic life, particularly for prayer and worship. It is "the meeting place. . . the retreat, the sanctuary, the center of society, and first and foremost, the House of Allah (God)." Additional contributors Kemal Korucu and Mirkena Ozer provide in

Appendix 2 a helpful statement about the early life of the Prophet Muhammad, builder of the first Mosque.

**Gareth Young** offers insightful perspective on the meditation or zazen as the practice of non-thinking at the Buddhist Zen Center. He says, "It is not a cutting off of thoughts and emptying of the mind – but allowing thoughts to arise, abide, and decay – observing them without engaging them." He verifies that the Zen Center fully embraces one of the essential restrictions of interfaith work – no proselytizing or conversion efforts – as evidenced by the sign outside the front door which reads: "All who enter here are welcome; none who leave are pursued."

**Mitch Cohen,** assisted by **Audrey Galex**, notes that the Synagogue is more than a place for communal worship. In fact, worship may not be prayer at all. Rather, it may be silence, taking in the energy of the sanctuary, or just being present in community. "What we pray doesn't always matter – shifting from our minds to our hearts in the Presence of G-d does," he wrote. He shared that in every Synagogue an Eternal Light burns which "reminds us that the Light of G-d, that spiritual energy, called by many names, is what all religions seek, even though that Light surrounds us at all times."

**Gillian Renault** opens the Hindu chapter in that same spirit, quoting the Rig Veda: "Truth is one, sages call it by many names." As is true with each contributor, she brings readers inside her sacred spaces of the Vedanta Center and the Hindu Temple, and connects their sanctity with the sacredness of the human soul. She affirms the truth of the divine Hindu text which says, "Look inward to find the Divine. It is not accessible if you look outward."

The primary premise of the Interfaith Immersion is that when people come into your Faith home, walls of fear, misinformation, and even hate come down as bridges are built and doors are flung open. When we enter the sacred space of the other, without threat or fear of conversion or condemnation, an inner life and reality of the other becomes real to us, and interfaith dialogue, understanding and relationships emerge clothed in hope, inspiration, enlightenment and the opportunity for a better and greater world.

The beauty of this book goes far beyond the practical service of bringing the reader inside five sacred places and the religious rites practiced within. The beauty is multilateral and multifarious. No one intended to write a book. It was the Interfaith Immersion work and collaboration that enlivened the Pen. The contributors are not trained or vetted authors, but their love of their faith and their gift of sharing a story creates a resplendent work. The coordination was relaxed, utilizing only their Immersion experience and the nexus of the Sacred Space to connect their chapters, and still the book is focused and congruent. The distinctions of the spaces and religions are clear and apparent, yet underneath the diversities, in the depths of the wisdom, the spirituality, the meanings, and the faith and souls of the people, lives an undeniable connectivity and mutuality.

A story found herein perhaps best summarizes this book's theme. A devout man spent his entire life recording the names of deities. Just before his death, he wrote on the last page of his notebook only two words: One God.

*-The Writing Team*

# About the Authors

**Mitch Cohen** graduated from Georgia Tech in 1981 and has pursued a career as an environmental engineer/consultant and environmental insurance broker. He completed his Masters Degree in Judaic Studies from Siegal College of Judaic Studies, Cleveland,OH. He is the lay spiritual leader of Shalom B'Harim (Peace in the Mountains) in Dahlonega, GA, an unaffiliated congregation of about 50 families. Mitch is also Assistant Director of "The Israel Encounter," a non-profit organization that leads trips to Israel for interfaith couples raising Jewish children. **Audrey Galex**, assistant in writing this chapter, is a professional storyteller, personal historian/video biographer and broadcast television producer and reporter, currently serving as Executive Producer for Atlanta Interfaith Broadcasters. She holds a Master's Degree in Broadcast Journalism from Northwestern University and a degree in International Relations from American University.

**Tom Buchanan** serves as Director of Christian Education at Shallowford Presbyterian Church in northeast Atlanta. He graduated from Vanderbilt University with a B.A. in Anthropology. He went on to Princeton Theological Seminary, earned the Master of Divinity degree, and has worked in educational ministry for churches in New Jersey and Georgia. His particular teaching interests center on interfaith relations, spirituality and culture, and the search for meaning in a post-Christian, pluralistic age.

**Imam Plemon T. El-Amin** has given generously of himself in the conception and development of this book. Born in Atlanta, educated at Harvard, he has worked tirelessly to introduce his community to interfaith practices and the importance of "getting to know each other." He is Imam Emeritus of the Atlanta Masjid of Al-Islam. He is a founding Board Member of Faith Alliance of Metro Atlanta, 100 People of Faith, and the Interfaith Community Institute. He serves as Director of the World Pilgrims. He has devoted his life to community ministry, education and developing positive interfaith relations in Atlanta, Georgia.

**Gillian Renault** was born in the United Kingdom. She grew up in a religious family and attended a small, rural Anglican church as a child. She immigrated to the United States in 1970, living first in New York, then Los Angeles and, for the last 12 years, in Atlanta. In Los Angeles, she was drawn to the Buddhist path and followed its meditation practices for many years. She has now found a home in the Hindu tradition – also known as Vedic spirituality. Gillian is a devotee at the Vedanta Center of Atlanta and serves on their board. She is also on the board of directors of the Faith Alliance of Metro Atlanta. Professionally, Gillian worked in Los Angeles' entertainment industry for twenty years. In Atlanta she specializes in media and presentation training. She is also a mixed media artist and a sculptor.

**Gareth Young** is a Zen Buddhist priest practicing in the lineage of Matsuoka-Roshi and Zenkai Taiun Michael Elliston at the Atlanta Soto Zen Center, and he serves on the board of the Faith Alliance of Metropolitan Atlanta. Gareth is also a successful businessman and author; his first novel was published in 2009. A graduate of Jesus College, Oxford, in the United Kingdom, with an MA in mathematics, he is married and lives in Atlanta with his wife and two teenage children.

*Jewish Sacred Space*

# CHAPTER ONE

# The Synagogue: Sacred Space of Jews

————————

**Mitch Cohen**
**Audrey Galex, assistant**

**If you have never visited a synagogue** where Jews worship G-d, and study Torah and biblical texts, or shared a Seder in a Jewish home, you might feel a little strange about participating in either. My purpose in writing about Sacred Space is to remove any uncertainty by guiding you to an understanding of both[1].

When you walk inside a synagogue, you are not only stepping into a Jewish house of worship but you are also stepping into four thousand years of Jewish history. You will take the first step through the doors, just as Abram took his first step away from the land of his father to wander and seek the Presence of One G-d (Genesis 12:1-9). Just as Jacob built an altar at the place where he dreamed of angels going up and down from heaven to earth, symbolizing that G-d was in that very place (Genesis 28:11-22), the sanctuary is the place where Jews converse with G-d through prayer and song and G-d converses with Jews through the wisdom and guidance of the biblical texts. This conversation between the Divine and the human makes the ordinary space sacred.

I can make a good case that the tradition we call Judaism today began with the Creation story, culminating with the creation of Adam and Eve which is recorded in the opening verses of the book of Genesis in the Hebrew Bible (1:24-31; 2:5-9). I can make an even better case that the tradition began after

Noah received a few basic rules after the Flood and was told by G-d to begin the history of the world all over again (Genesis 8:15-22). Another case for the beginning of the tradition we today call Judaism might be the story of Abram mentioned above and his bringing forth the belief in One G-d.

Rabbi Harold Kushner wrote in his book *To Life* that ". . . if Genesis is the basic biblical statement about what G-d wants and needs from human beings in general, (the book of) Exodus is the definitive statement about G-d's relationship . . . (with the Israelites). It tells the story of how an anonymous band of slaves was transformed into the nation that taught the human race about the one G-d."[2]

Therefore, I think that perhaps the best case for the tradition we today call Judaism might well be the Exodus story. Around three thousand years ago, the Israelites, shortly after being freed from slavery in Egypt, encountered G-d at Mount Sinai. The relationship between G-d and the Israelites was established, G-d providing both the physical and spiritual sustenance and the Israelites creating a society according to the laws and guidance set forth at Sinai and given to Moses. Wandering in the wilderness for forty more years before entering Canaan, the Israelites established a civilization based on the teachings at Sinai (which we'll reference as the Torah) and the practices performed in the Temple built by King Solomon. Like many of the ancient Near Eastern religions, the Israelites centered religious worship around the Temple and the offering of sacrifices. The Israelites regularly brought animals to the Temple as offerings of gratitude and well-being and to provide atonement for unintentional and intentional transgressions against the teachings of the Torah.[3]

Just a couple of hundred years after establishing the Israelite monarchy, the Israelites split into two kingdoms, Israel in the north and Judah in the south. The Assyrians destroyed the northern Kingdom of Israel in 722 BCE, while the Babylonians destroyed the southern Kingdom of Judea along with the Temple in Jerusalem in 586 BCE.[4] With no Temple at which to sacrifice, what were the Israelites to do? About forty-seven years after the destruction of the Temple, the Persians conquered Babylon and allowed the Israelites to return to Jerusalem to rebuild the Second Temple. However, the need for another form of "sacrifice" had been born from necessity.[5]

As stated earlier, synagogues as permanent places of communal gathering for prayer likely originated in Babylon after the destruction of the first Temple and the exile of the Israelites to Babylon. After they returned from Babylonian exile, their congregational worship, which consisted of prayer and the study of biblical stories, passed down as the tradition. Jewish law and history developed side by side with the revival of the sacrificial rituals of the Second Temple in Jerusalem. The idea of a communal gathering for prayer and study other than at the Temple led to the building of synagogues across Judea and later in other places across the Jewish Diaspora. (Diaspora refers to Jews scattered throughout the nations.)

When you enter a modern synagogue, you might be surprised that, apart from modern architecture, the basic layout is similar to a synagogue built in the Diaspora at least two thousand years ago, if not more. One of the first things you'll notice about two-thirds of the way up the right doorpost is a *mezuzah*; the mezuzah encases a scroll containing the text of Deuteronomy 6:4-9 and 11:13-21. This text inside includes the most important Jewish declaration, which we call the Shema, "Hear O Israel, the Eternal is our G-d, the Eternal is One," along with other texts such as, "Love your G-d with all your heart and with all your soul....Take to heart these instructions: teach them to your children... inscribe them on the doorpost of your house and on your gates...." For us, the mezuzah is a Jewish touchstone, reminding us that we are entering a holy place. It also reminds us that there is a set of ethical and moral guidelines within which even the most liberal Jews should consider in daily living. Most importantly, the mezuzah also reminds us that there is a Higher Power, a Creative, Endless and Eternal One who connects all living things and to whom we commit to use our gifts and talents to make the world a better place for all.

Once inside the synagogue, you'll see places for worshippers to sit, always facing a Holy Ark that contains the Torah, the five books of Moses, which are also the first five books of the Christian Bible. The Holy Ark is a reminder of the biblical ark that was used to carry the two tables of the Covenant through the Wilderness about 3,200 years ago. The Holy Ark was also the central object of worship in the Temple.[6] There is a seven-stem menorah, or candelabra (Exodus 25:31-40), which is the oldest symbol of Judaism – not the Star of David, which might not even be of Jewish origin, though the Star of David was used at least two thousand years ago during the Roman rule of Jewish Jerusalem.[7] More traditional Jews believe that Moses received the entire Torah and oral law (traditional interpretations and legal rendering, which later became the Talmud) on top of Sinai.[8] More progressive Jews believe that only the Ten Commandments were received by Moses on Sinai. The Torah scroll is handwritten to this day by scribes on parchment and rolled in the same manner in which it was scribed at least two thousand years ago.

Above the Holy Ark, a light stays lit perpetually. We call this the Eternal Light, and it symbolizes "a lamp to burn continually" in the Wilderness tabernacle as a physical Presence of G-d (Exodus 27:20-21).[9] To me, the Eternal Light also represents the first day of creation, the Divine Spiritual Light with which the Universe was created, the eternal spiritual Presence of G-d. Seeing the flickering Eternal Light above the Ark reminds us that the Light of G-d, that spiritual energy called by many names, is what all religions seek, even though that Light surrounds us at all times.

Our prayer service is embodied in a formal liturgy with chants and prayers taken directly from the Torah, Psalms and songs that relate to the Exodus drama. There are prayers that remind Jews of their responsibility through observing commandments; these prayers inspire us to make the world the kind of place that G-d wishes it to be. There are set prayers following a set liturgy for weekday, Sabbath and festival services in the prayerbook, known as a *Siddur*.[10] There is also a special prayerbook for the High Holiday liturgy (*Rosh Hashanah* – the Jewish New Year and *Yom Kippur* – the Day of Atonement). In the more progressive Jewish movements (more on the different movements later in this chapter) there can also be places in the service for personal prayer and even silent meditation.

The synagogue is more than a place for communal worship, and worship might not be prayer. For example, some Jews attend a service and never open a prayerbook – they just want to be in community with their own silent meditations. They might study a Torah commentary or might sit silently, drawing in the energy of the sanctuary, listening to remembered melodies from childhood. Just being present in community inside the synagogue can be almost as important as formal prayer itself. While individual prayer is one of the ways a Jew communicates with G-d, community is so important that Jews must gather at least ten people over the age of thirteen to have an "acceptable" service.[11]

Hebrew is the language of Jewish prayer. Across all Jewish movements, from the most fundamental (Orthodox) to the most progressive (Reform), a Jewish prayer will be recited or chanted either entirely or partly in Hebrew. As Rabbi Harold Kushner wrote, hearing Hebrew when one does not understand it forces the reader or listener to use his or her right brain, the brain of creativity. Therefore, many of us believe that a Jewish prayer service is not really about the words – it is about the service sparking an emotional and aesthetic experience.[12] What we pray doesn't always matter – shifting from our minds to our hearts in the Presence of G-d does matter. I've been taught that prayer is humanity

**18**

communicating with G-d, while G-d communicates with humans through the symbolic and allegoric messages of the biblical texts. As you worship in a synagogue, you'll find that the service is as much about sharing ourselves at the deepest level with G-d through the liturgy, as it is about silent and spontaneous personal prayer and meditation.

Like the Torah and the prayerbook, the Talmud is another very important text for Jews. It is literature, commentary and legal renderings that clarify confusing, incomplete and even contradictory texts in the Torah. For example, what does "be fruitful and multiply" really mean (this is considered the very first commandment)? How do you "remember and observe the Sabbath" ? These texts and many others are debated and defined in the Talmud. There is a teaching that when one establishes a new village or city, the first structure built must be a *mikveh*, or ritual bath, and then a school. The school is so important because Jews believe that G-d's lessons and desires for humanity are hidden in the biblical texts and we need to seek them out. One must know how to read in order to "hear" G-d.

We consider study to be a form of worship and an important part of Jewish life. Contrary to the stereotype, Jews are not any smarter than any other group – we just tend to be more educated. We are brought up to question everything and reading/studying Torah is done at least every Sabbath, as well as on certain holidays. Torah study involves personally sharing interpretations of the text and also sharing life experiences related to the text being considered. The sharing of the community is as important as a scholar or rabbi sharing his or her views or even drawing from the commentaries of Torah scholars from the distant past. Yes, disagreeing or seeing things differently from the rabbi is allowed and encouraged.

The Torah is divided into portions and a reading/study is done every Sabbath, with the goal being to read the entire Torah in one year. The Torah is also read on Mondays and Thursdays in more traditional congregations. The prayer service is a combination of formal communal prayers and some informal times of personal prayer and reflection. The service follows a liturgy established in one of the first prayerbooks at least twelve hundred years ago.[13] What you may notice during a typical service is that several worshippers may be chanting Hebrew prayers at different speeds, other people may be talking, some may be doing various forms of body movements, and still others may be reading from the English translation of the prayers. You might see children running up the aisles and people talking aloud to each other. These multiple activities may be disconcerting, especially if you are used to a quiet, directed service in which everyone follows the service leader. In Judaism being present with others is almost more important than the prayers, so the different activities in the sanctuary are not a distraction. A rabbi and/or cantor (trained to sing or chant the liturgy) typically leads a service, though a lay person may also lead any service.

Jews come to worship services for varying reasons. I heard about a Jew who came to his services every Sabbath and never opened a prayerbook. He used the entire service to listen to the melodies of his youth, to disconnect from the hectic life of his profession and to be with other people who also were seeking to get "unplugged" from their work worlds. I imagine that many Jews sometimes just stare through the windows at the trees, the sky and the clouds – being one with nature is a form of gratitude prayer. For many this is a deeply religious experience. I, too, have found it such.

The sound of music fills many sanctuaries in today's synagogues – some only by human voice according to tradition and others accompanied by musical instruments. More traditional synagogues do not allow musical instruments to be played on Sabbath as adherence to the prohibition against work on Sabbath and as a way to continue mourning the destruction of the Temple.[14] The more progressive synagogues interpret the Sabbath prohibitions more liberally and allow the playing of instruments to bring joy and praise to Sabbath, as stated in Psalms 92 ("... It is good to praise the Eternal...with a ten-stringed harp, with voice and lyre together") and 150 ("...praise G-d with blasts of the horn; praise G-d with harp and lyre..."). On Sabbath, traditional congregations do not allow photography or videography, and they also prohibit the use of cellphones, videogames and other electronic devices either in the sanctuary or in the synagogue on Sabbath.[15] This will likely be the case in many progressive synagogues as well.

Dress in a synagogue is modest, and almost all men and some women wear head coverings or hats. The head coverings are known in Hebrew as *kippot* (singular is *kippah* or, in Yiddish, the *yarmulke*). Even the Pope wears a kippah!

When you visit a synagogue, you will likely observe men, and in some cases women, wearing the *tallit* or prayer shawl. The *tallit* has fringes on the four corners. The description of fringes on the corners of one's garment comes from the Torah (Numbers 15:38, Deuteronomy 22:12).[16] The only parts of the *tallit* that have spiritual significance are the fringes on the four corners. Each fringe, known as a *tzitzit*, has one string wrapped around seven strings, with rows of wraps separated by five knots.[17] Wearing a *tallit* reminds the wearer of the commandments and the commitments that guide Jewish life; it also reminds us that our life is centered in the one G-d.[18]

There are no special requirements, no secret passwords, no knowledge of Hebrew or Jewish liturgy, nor is written permission needed, for anyone to come to a Jewish service. There is no need to even understand what goes on during the service. All that is necessary is the desire to be around others seeking to experience the Presence of G-d. This Presence can be felt by just closing your eyes and listening to the other worshippers chant in unison, an ancient language that brings any worshipper or visitor back to the foot of Mount Sinai or the place of any life-altering Revelation of Wisdom that guides one's life.

## The Other Sacred Space: The Home

The synagogue is just one physical space in which Jewish spirituality unfolds. The worship space in the synagogue has an air of holiness, but the worship space in the home is just as holy. Jewish homes are as important as synagogues in creating spiritual space. We perform numerous rituals in the home, with the *seder*, which is an order of prayers and rituals for Sabbath, being the most practiced home ritual.

## Sabbath

At sunset each Friday, we light candles and then say a blessing acknowledging the commandment to light Sabbath candles to bring in Sabbath. We light at least two Sabbath candles, which are symbolic of several things. The two candles represent the commandment to "remember" the Sabbath and "keep it holy" (Exodus 20:8). Mystically, the light of the candles also represents the spiritual Light of the first day of creation.[19] And mystically, the view of G-d manifested in the physical world as male and female emanations is represented by the two candles.

We use wine as a religious symbol of joy and sanctification, so we say a blessing over the wine to acknowledge our gratitude toward G-d for creating the fruit of the vine. In fact, in home worship we sanctify just about everything with wine and a blessing.

In Jewish history, Judaism's survival has always been dependent upon the children who carry forward the teaching passed to them from generation to generation. We therefore bless our children during the Sabbath seder, which symbolizes the completeness and importance of a cohesive and loving Jewish family. Husbands also bless their wives.

Just like the manna that G-d provided to the Israelites wandering in the desert, our bodies must be nourished to survive. We wash our hands and then say a blessing over the challah, the traditional braided egg bread, as a closing Sabbath *seder* ritual, which signifies gratitude for the grains that come forth from the earth. Interestingly, the blessing for the challah again infers our cooperation with G-d. We interpret the blessing in that G-d brings forth the grain from the earth, and yet we humans must make the flour, knead the dough and bake the bread. With this interpretation, we realize that G-d needs us and we need G-d. Following a festive Sabbath dinner, many families and friends celebrate Sabbath at home or in the synagogue by singing Sabbath songs.

Special memories about the Sabbath observance remain central to Audrey's continued connection to Judaism. She recalls:

*We were seated around the Sabbath dinner table at the apartment of my paternal grandmother, whom we called Sugie (like sugar.) Every week, the meal would consist of something like: chopped liver, challah, vegetables for an appetizer; roasted chicken and green vegetables, along with tzimmis (a succulent mix of sweet potatoes, carrots, maple syrup, short ribs, etc.) and maybe kishke (stuffed derma that would make a cardiologist cringe – full of chicken fat, fried onions and other unhealthy morsels). And then there was dessert -- cakes and cookies and pies Sug tailor-made for each of her grandchildren (yours truly got an apple pie, which I make to this day.) The evening would begin with our dad chanting the blessing over wine (Sug would have lit the candles already: she was particular about lighting them according to tradition, 18 minutes before sundown). The kids would lead the prayer over the challah and then there would occur another ritual: My dad would declare (miraculously, every week) that this was the best chopped liver, ever. The laughter, the misbehavior, the prayers, the conversation around that table, the neighbors dropping in for a visit -- all contribute to the mosaic of Sabbath ritual memories. Those Sabbath dinners and the ritual of prayer and community – the ritual provided the structure for the magic and mystery of the Divine to dwell amongst us.*

My favorite memory of Sabbath is the time that I sat in the dark with my grandmother, who in those latter years was lost in a fog of dementia. The lights in the kitchen were off, and we sat there with only the light of the candles glowing and reflecting off of our faces. My grandmother did not know who

I was, yet she felt compelled to share a vivid memory of being a little girl in Belarus and going to Hebrew school. She recalled a *pogrom* (a Russian word for violent rampage), where the women and children grabbed the Sabbath *menorah* (candle holder), *kiddush* cup (ritual cup for blessing the wine) and perhaps the *Chanukiah* (Chanukah menorah) and then hid in the cellar while the attackers burned the village. Though the memory was haunting, it connected me to my grandmother and our shared history.

## Havdallah

*Havdallah*, another beautiful service, ends the Sabbath and can be performed at home or preferably outside in nature under the first three stars of Saturday evening. *Havdallah*, which means separation in Hebrew, pertains to the separation of Sabbath from the beginning of the new week. It is a service made up of four prayers, ritual objects and at least one song.[20]

The *Havdallah* candle is comprised of at least three braided candles that join at the twisted wick and is lit to start the service. Some say that the braided candle represents the strength and diversity of the Jewish people and even perhaps the diversity of the intertwined world in which Jews live. The first *Havdallah* prayer is made for an overflowing cup of wine, as wine is used to sanctify and bless G-d's creation. The overflowing cup symbolizes our wish for the overflow of blessings of Sabbath into the coming week. The second *Havdallah* prayer is over a ritual spice box filled with the most fragrant of spices. At the end of Sabbath, a sense of sadness is felt as we get ready to return to the work week. The smell of the spices is meant to gladden our sadness over the end of Sabbath. The third *Havdallah* prayer is for the braided candle. The flame of the *Havdallah* candle symbolizes the separation of the spiritual world of Sabbath from the material world into which participants are about to engage in the new week. My favorite modern ritual concerning the *Havdallah* is to form a circle around the person holding the candle for the entire service while everyone holds up their hands so that the light is reflected off of their fingernails to the people opposite them. This symbolizes the interconnectedness of us all, as we send the reflected light of the candle across to each other all the way around the circle. To me, this is a form of blessing the other with more spiritual Light as we embark on the new week. The fourth prayer is actually the prayer of separation from Sabbath and back to the work week, the separation of the Holy and the secular.[21]

## Chanukah

Lighting Chanukah candles on each of the eight nights of Chanukah and participating in a communal Passover Seder are two other important spiritual, family-centered practices conducted in a Jewish home. Chanukah is always an exciting occasion, as we celebrate with family, including extended family. Lighting the candles signifies the miraculous victory of a small group of Jewish zealots, known as the Macabees, against the overwhelming larger Greek-Assyrian war machine in 164 BCE.[22] The defiled Temple was restored and rededicated, which allowed the Jews to reinstate the making of sacrifices. The Talmud teaches that the eight candles lit successively, one for each of the eight days of Chanukah, represents the miracle of the oil lamp in the rededicated Temple that should have lasted one day, but instead lasted all eight days (Talmud [Gemara], tractate Sabbath 21 [ Masechet Sabbath]).

Celebrating with our extended family, no matter how distant our cousins might be, is a tradition that came from Europe, or perhaps it is a tradition that resulted from two thousand years of exile. Confined to ghettos, Jews could only depend on each other for survival. Chanukah offers a family holiday of hope, religious freedom and triumph against all odds. This festive event is celebrated entirely in the Jewish home. We eat foods cooked in oil as part of the celebration, and we suspend diets during Chanukah, as we also eat jelly doughnuts and potato latkes (pancakes), mainstays of the Jewish Chanukah table.

My favorite Chanukah memories center on the last few years of my father's life. My brother, sister, wife, our three sons, my cousin and his family and my parents would cram into their condo and light the menorah together. We would eat potato latkes, apple sauce, sour cream and even pizza for those who just could not eat another latke. We even brought some jelly doughnuts. Afterward, my father would sit in his favorite chair and watch as the grandchildren and each of his grown children, his nephew and extended family opened gifts. I never saw such joy on my father's face. Because he had grown up poor and struggled financially for many years, joining this celebration with his family filled him with great happiness. The gifts didn't matter – it was seeing his family with the light of the menorah glowing in the background that brought him such joy.

**Passover**

Passover commemorates the exodus of the Hebrew slaves from Egypt (Ex 14) about thirty-two hundred years ago (1200 BCE), and it is a springtime celebration.[23] It is an eight-day celebration in the Diaspora (seven days in Israel), and it starts with a ritual and festive meal known as a Passover Seder (Exodus 12; Talmud tractate Pesachim). During Passover, Jews eat unleavened bread, or matzah, and refrain from eating leavened foods.[24]

A favorite Passover memory of mine was being part of the Seder at the home of my Aunt Pearl and Uncle Stanley. I was about six years old, and the kitchen was so small that the family did the Seder in shifts – children first and then adults. My grandmother, who was still very lucid, made the best chicken soup with matzah balls. It was exciting to eat the soup until I could see the clown imprinted on the bottom of the soup bowl. It turned out that the Passover soup bowl was the same one used by my mother when she was a little girl. I also felt so grown up because I was allowed to drink a little of the Passover wine with seltzer (soda water) mixed in. I remember how good it felt being the next cousin in line to chant the four questions in Hebrew, which is an important part of the Seder that re-enacts a child asking their parents four important questions about the meaning of Passover. Those four questions are: 1) Why do we eat only matzah on Pesach and not all kinds of breads like other nights? 2) Why do we eat bitter herbs at our Seder? 3) At our Seder, why do we dip herbs twice (typically romaine lettuce and horseradish dipped in "brick mortar" made of apples, walnuts and wine)? 4) Why do we lean on a pillow while eating tonight and do not sit straight like other nights?

A Passover memory of Audrey's took place around the seder table where many Jewish memories are created. She writes: *"I had just completed my first semester and a half of college, away from home. At one point in the seder, there must have been a lull in conversation, when I turned to my father and confessed in full voice that I had decided to become a Sufi Muslim, an adherent of the mystical tradition of Islam. Thinking he would perhaps become agitated and send me to my room, I was wrong. Instead, he calmly looked at me and said, 'Young lady, keep reading.' Many years later, with college-age children of my own, I am convinced his words reflect the value of study and internal reflection, as well as struggle, over Jewish spirituality and expression."*

## Home as a Temple

It should be no surprise that the Jewish home is a mini-representation of a Temple, with rituals and ritual objects displayed throughout. Even non-practicing Jews will typically hang a *mezuzah* on the right doorpost of their home, about two-thirds of the way up and pointing in. Spiritually, the *mezuzah* is a Jewish reminder to those entering that they are coming inside another Jewish holy place – the Jewish home. Each day as I leave my home, I am reminded that my day is supported by the wisdom and guidelines of a long Jewish tradition.

## Life beyond the Synagogue and the Home

Beyond the synagogue and home we live our lives among others in what we generally regard as a broken, struggling world. Here we live out the demands of our faith; here we learn in our own experience that our lives have meaning beyond ourselves. What then is this Jewish spirituality?

Jewish belief and spirituality reflect a complex and broad spectrum of faith – from belief in a G-d that is omnipotent, omnipresent, and in control of everything; a G-d who created everything, but who also takes a hands-off approach to the laws of nature and man's free-will choice[25]; G-d as non-anthropomorphic but rather a force/energy that acts for good in the world; to not much belief in G-d at all. With such a wide expression of belief/non-belief in G-d, it is no surprise that Judaism is more a behavior-based religion than a faith-based religion – there is no Jewish creed.

## Aspects of faith and practice

Many modern Jews, especially here in the U.S., identify themselves as secular. Their Jewish identity is comprised of a connection to Jewish history, art, food, humor and an emphasis on Jewish ethics and responsible choices of behavior -- but not a clear sense of who or what G-d is. After all, the Hebrew word *Israel* means one who wrestles with G-d and is taken from the story of Jacob wrestling with a Divine being (Genesis 32:24-30). Many believe that Jacob was actually wrestling with his own spiritual doubts and his relationship with G-d. Therefore, it would be appropriate to say that Jews are still Israelites (and so is anyone of any religion who struggles with what G-d is and how they relate to G-d). We continue to wrestle with what we believe about G-d and yet we focus on the choices we make, the actions we take and how regardless of what we believe about G-d, that in some manner we are G-d's hands in the physical world, doing the things that G-d wants us to do to make an imperfect and flawed world more complete.

So, while Jews are all over the board with respect to what G-d is, how G-d acts in the world and what we believe about G-d, it was Judaism that first brought to the world the idea of One Supreme Creative Entity. According to the book of Genesis, G-d was first known as "El Shaddai" – usually interpreted as G-d Almighty (Genesis 17:1). However, there are two main Hebrew words used mostly in the Hebrew Bible for the name of the One G-d: *Eloheinu* (our G-d) and *Adonai*.

Jewish tradition interprets these two names used most frequently in the Hebrew Bible and in the liturgy as aspects of G-d: Elohim represents the aspect of Divine justice, and *Adonai* (traditionally interpreted as Lord) represents Divine mercy or grace. While nobody can explain why bad things happen to good people, some would believe that everything happens according to G-d's will. This is a more traditional view and may very well be a minority Jewish view. I defer to Rabbi Harold Kushner, who wrote in *When Bad Things Happen to Good People* that G-d may not be omnipotent and takes a hands off approach to the free will of humans and the laws of nature. In Kushner's Jewish view, illness is caused by bad biology that is benignly indifferent to man, not caused by a punitive G-d.[26] In this view, G-d did NOT create Hurricane Katrina to cause much death and destruction as punishment to the people of New Orleans – nature's weather systems and patterns caused it.

However, Rabbi Kushner also writes that G-d always shows up in the healing that happens after the losses and tragedies in our lives, most often through the work and loving support of other human beings. We do eventually heal. I can certainly say that my healing from my father's death was directly a result of the support of my community, plus a great book that guided me through the year-long Jewish mourning process and a wonderful therapist. Compassion is an innate gift to man from G-d. It is through us that G-d works providing Divine Grace so that man eventually transcends his challenges, and survives his losses and suffering.

## Divine Mercy

Divine mercy or grace is an integral part of Jewish belief – but not as reward. G-d is a patient Creator who cares deeply for all living things. G-d knows and takes into account human frailty and fallibility, yet still holds man in the highest regard.

## Live in the Now – Life is No Dress Rehearsal

As previously stated, Judaism is a tradition of deeds and not of creeds. It is lived in the present with little or no emphasis on preparing for life after death. Since Jews believe that the soul is eternal and that the body is finite, life after death is a given for all human beings, not just Jews. In fact, Jews do not really prepare for the Afterlife. According to Jewish teaching, life is to be lived in the present, using all of our gifts to reach our highest potential in the service of humanity and G-d. If we do this, the Afterlife takes care of itself.

Neither do we believe in an eternally burning Hell. Perhaps the closest idea is what tradition refers to as *Gehenna*, which is similar to the Catholic doctrine of Purgatory.[27] In one teaching from the Jewish perspective, at death the soul departs the body and enters *Gehenna*, where it goes through a process of purification and purgation before eventually entering the *Gan Eden* (Garden of Eden, or Heaven) to be in the Presence of G-d.[28] There is a Talmudic tradition that says that it should take about a year for a soul to make it through *Gehenna* (*tractate Sabbath 33b*)[29]. However, when we chant a special mourning prayer, which we call the *mourner's kaddish*, we can help hasten the journey of the departed soul to Higher Realms.[30] So, you may now be asking, "what about Hitler – did he have a 'get out of jail' card - certainly as a Jew you must not believe that Hitler goes to Heaven?" There are some who say that the most wicked human beings who made really bad and evil choices in their lives never make it out of *Gehenna* and are always separated from the Divine Presence. I guess that is as close to a belief in hell as Jews can get. However, many of us believe that hell is created right here on Earth and we are responsible for creating it – through our acts of greed, hate, violence, deceit, dishonesty, etc.[31]

From the Jewish mystical tradition we even have a belief in reincarnation. However, the Jewish mystical view of reincarnation is not a reward – it is what happens when we do not live our lives according to the Divine mission we are assigned just before birth – correcting the wrongdoings from our previous

28

life, sort of like unfinished "homework assignments" given to us when the soul enters the new body. Rather than the reward of the soul being in G-d's Presence, we have to come back with the opportunity to do it again until we fulfill our mission, complete our "assignments" and fully develop the soul. Some "perfected" souls come back by choice, to guide others, similar to the Buddhist bodhisattva.[32] According to Rabbi Byron Sherwin, until the late 1600s belief in Jewish mystical practices, including reincarnation or transmigration of souls, was a predominant theology among Jews.[33] Presently, reincarnation is not a belief held by a majority of modern Jews; however, a number of us, including myself, believe in reincarnation enough to fill workshops on Jewish mysticism.

What drives serious Jews are Jewish guidelines, which influence their choices, actions and deeds. Jews refer to these guidelines as *mitzvot*, or commandments. In Judaism, moral commandments are those that Jews believe would have us behave in ways that make us relate most to G-d, such as the dietary laws (i.e., man can control his instinct to eat anything he desires), observance of the Sabbath (i.e., ceasing work, as G-d did after reaching a stopping point in the act of creation). Some simple examples of the ethical commandments are prohibitions against stealing, murder, dealing dishonestly, and obligations such as taking care of the widow, the orphan and the poor. It would not be a stretch to say that all of the ethical commandments in Judaism would work for anyone of any religion. Moral and ethical commandments all help the serious Jew to constantly choose between inclinations toward good or selfishness/evil in how they treat people and conduct business. Commandments are the boundaries to the playing field of life for the serious Jew – whether the commandments are adhered to most traditionally or liberally.

There is a *midrash*, a story that relates to biblical text or law that illustrates what Jews believe about how one should treat others and how we create Heaven or hell on Earth. There are many versions of this tale. Here is one:

*A man died and appeared before a majestic palace. He entered and looked to the first chamber on the left where he saw a huge dining table with platters of the most wonderful food imaginable. Seeing what he knew must have been a feast, he thought he was in Heaven. Then, he looked at the people sitting around the table. He was shocked to see they were emaciated, despondent and frightened. Then he noticed all had steel bands strapped to their elbows that did not allow them to bend their arms. They struggled to reach the forkfuls of wonderful food to their mouths, but none could. The food simply fell off the forks, and onto the floor.*

*The man then went to the chamber on the right. He again saw a table full of the most wonderful food imaginable. Again, he saw people around the table with bands around their elbows. But something was odd. Instead of emaciated bodies, these people appeared full-figured and joyful. It was then that he observed the reason. As each person filled his fork with food, he turned and fed his neighbor. Now, he knew he was in Heaven.*

## Meditation

Meditation has been part of Jewish practice for thousands of years, though it is not widely known or widely practiced by most Jews. Abraham Abulafia was a Jewish mystic from Spain in the mid-1200s. Rabbi Byron Sherwin wrote that Abulafia developed meditative techniques that may have been influenced by other religious traditions, such as Christianity, Islamic Sufism and Hinduism.[34] In a mantra-like Jewish meditation the practitioner chants a Hebrew prayer, phrase or words that have particular meaning. Many simply repeat the word *shalom*, which means hello, goodbye and peace, with an emphasis on peace. Note how coincidentally shalom ends with an *–om*, just as in the famous Hindu meditative chant, *ohm*. Even the repetitive bending forward and back movement during Jewish prayer can be a kinesthetic meditation. Therefore, meditation reaches across all spiritual traditions in the similar way that all meditation helps to silence the chatter in our minds, so that we can hear the small inner voice within our hearts.

## Four Expressions of Judaism

By now, you've read the terms "Traditional" and "Progressive" in my description of Jewish observances. Therefore, in order to better understand Jewish spirituality and beliefs, let's first seek a basic understanding of the four major Jewish movements – Orthodox, Reform, Conservative, and Reconstructionist.

## Orthodox Judaism

Traditional Judaism mostly refers to Orthodox Judaism and means the strict observance of Jewish law, which legislates all modes of Jewish behavior described through Divine revelation as the commandments in the Torah (and clarified, codified and explained in the Talmud).[35] This strict adherence applies to many aspects of daily life, such as the dietary laws, purity rituals for married women, how to conduct business, civil/ criminal law, synagogue/prayer rituals and practices, and Sabbath and holy day observances. Jewish mystics also retained tradition and believed (and still believe) that strict adherence to Jewish law and the commandments is the path to redeeming a broken world that is imperfect, thus amplifying G-d's Presence. For the Jewish mystic, each commandment performed, such as showing gratitude through saying a blessing, doing good deeds, performing acts of loving kindness, brings humanity one step closer to the Messianic Age.[36]

## Reform Judaism

In the first half of the 1800s, as a response to the Great Enlightenment that began spreading from France across Europe, early reformers of traditional Judaism founded the Reform Jewish movement, with its roots and strongest presence in Germany. Reform Judaism attempted to interpret the commandments liberally so as to adapt to the views and life of modernity.[37] The reformers emphasized the ethical commandments and placed less emphasis on the ritual commandments, which included rejecting the dietary laws. Once Reform Judaism made its way across the Atlantic to the United States, it spread rapidly.

## Conservative Judaism

The Conservative movement began in the late 1800s. Conservative Jews believed that the reformers had gone too far and that the Orthodox strict adherence to Jewish law was perhaps outdated. Unlike Reform Judaism, Conservative Jews feel bound by almost all of the Torah rituals and Torah ethics; however, they also feel free to bring a modern approach to Jewish law. It could be said that Conservative Judaism combines "tradition and change" and that Jewish law definitely has a vote in everyday modern life, although not a total veto.[38]

## Reconstructionist Judaism

The fourth major movement is the smallest, Reconstructionism, whose founding is credited to Mordechai Kaplan. Kaplan accepted that the Jewish rituals were more "folkways" than divine commandments.[39] He felt that the power of Judaism was in the community – not in the institutions, not even synagogues. Kaplan encouraged the creation of smaller, intimate Jewish spiritual communities, called *Havurot*, similar to what Christians refer to as fellowship groups.[40]  Kaplan liked Jewish tradition, yet he wanted the spiritual power to lie more with the people than with a distant G-d.

Today, you'll find the lines between the four movements – Reform, Reconstructionist, Conservative and Orthodox – can be blurred, yet the defining point of distinction is typically how Jewish law is applied within each community and at each synagogue.  Reform Judaism would still be the most liberal of the movements and Orthodox Judaism the most traditional. Conservative and Reconstructionist would fall somewhere between Reform and Orthodox.

Three Progressive Synagogue Experiences:  Reconstructionist, Reform and Conservative.  At an Atlanta Reconstructionist Congregation, Sabbath services usually begin with a niggun, or wordless melody, to gather people together and quiet the worshippers. Sabbath candles are lit and the prayers begin, often infused with music, chanting, meditation and drumming.  Many of the songs reflect diversity within the Jewish experience – different races, different ethnicities and different sexual orientations, from melodies emerging out of the Mediterranean cultures, to songs and tunes from India and Africa.

The rabbi often invites comments from the congregation during his sermon.  The service ends as it started, with a song that brings people to their feet, with arms around each other's shoulders.

Following the service, people gather in the social hall to sing together the blessing over the wine.  The *challah* is then blessed, with everyone holding to one of two loaves, and/or holding to the shoulder or arm of someone who's holding the *challah* to form a chain of connection.

On Saturday, people engage in a Torah discussion, while munching on bagels and cream cheese.  Discussion is lively, with a wide range of views/debates on just about any topic.

At a typical Reform synagogue the cantor, who plays piano, and the cantorial soloist (who plays guitar) supports the rabbi in welcoming the Sabbath with song.  Like many Reform congregations, the community likes to sing *with* the clergy and not to be sung to – services are not a performance, but a musical experience shared by all. Many modern musical versions of traditional psalms and prayers are now standard during the service.  At several Reform synagogues, there is an occasional "Friday Night Live" service, in which a klezmer band (traditional eastern European Jewish band) or group of instrumentalists sing the entire service to the music of Jewish musical artist Craig Taubman.  At each of the synagogues there is time for personal prayer and meditation during the service, and the rabbi's sermon is inspiring and interactive, often created around a song lyric or even a sports reference to drive the spiritual lesson of the sermon home. After services, the cantor leads the blessings over the wine and *challah*, and then everyone convenes in the social hall to connect, reconnect, talk or just share time bringing in the Sabbath with cookies, pastries, fruit and other goodies.

At a local Conservative synagogue, the Friday evening service follows the traditional liturgy; however, one of the rabbis plays beautiful classical guitar and leads the opening psalms to the music of Shlomo Carlbach, a traditional Jew who brought music to the traditional Friday liturgy. It is very unusual for a Conservative synagogue to allow the guitar; however, this is not the typical Conservative synagogue – there are two rabbis, a wonderful husband and wife team. Although the Carlbach melodies accompany the chanting of psalms, there are also traditional Hebrew reading and chanting of the main part of the service, accompanied by the classical guitar. Toward the end of the service, children are brought up to stand under the protective canopy of a large *tallit*, a prayer shawl held by adult members of the congregation, as one of the rabbis chants the traditional Priestly Blessing (Numbers 6:23-27) to bless each of the children.

Women have begun to reclaim, redefine and reconstruct spiritual practices, including rewriting and using gender-neutral language in prayer and liturgy. In some homes, recent Passover practices reflect a new spiritual consciousness of the feminine: the use of a cup of spring water to represent the Prophetess Miriam, alongside Elijah's Cup filled with wine; the placing of an orange on the Passover seder plate to reflect and reject the words attributed to a prominent traditional rabbi who once suggested that welcoming women on the pulpit as clergy is as absurd as an orange on the seder plate. Women have also reclaimed connections to public ritual practice with the monthly "New Moon" observance. During this ritual, some gather to immerse themselves in the "*mikveh*" or ritual bath of spiritual renewal. Some gather to share stories of their emerging womanhood, either with peers, and/or along with their daughters. Many more women are answering the call of spiritual seeking by assuming leadership positions, both on and off the pulpit.

## What Jews have to offer to the interfaith community

Regardless of what the many religious traditions believe, or do not believe, about G-d, it was Judaism that introduced the idea of One G-d to the world.   Both Christianity and Islam believe in this same One G-d, though they may access the presence of this G-d in different ways.   Even religions that do not believe in one G-d can relate to the Jewish idea that humans are most like G-d through their actions and deeds. These deeds encourage our fellow human beings to reach their highest potential so that they can contribute to others and make a better world.  Since Judaism does not insist that it is the only pathway to G-d, visitors, explorers or spiritual seekers will not be made to feel inadequate or wrong in their own beliefs.

The ritual objects in a synagogue – the Holy Ark and Torah – are tied to four thousand years of Jewish history, as are the eternal light above the Holy Ark and the seven-stem menorah, often found in a synagogue. Facing towards Jerusalem, the holiest place in Judaism, speaks to Christians, as well as Muslims, since Jerusalem is also sacred to them. This shared vision of God provides a basis for significant discussion.

In addition to faith in the one God and a shared view of the world, there is also a commonality of liturgy. For Christians, there is a sense of familiarity with the liturgy of a Jewish service, even the prayers that are read or chanted.  Many Christian prayers derive from the Torah, Psalms and books of Prophets, which comprise the Hebrew Bible.  Of course, the Five Books of Moses (the Torah) are included in the Christian Old Testament.

To the interfaith conversation, Judaism also brings a method of studying sacred texts.  Jewish study is not preaching, nor is it dictatorial; rather, it is studying together *with the teacher*. Arguing the texts dates back to the Talmudic period at least 1,800 years ago, when scholars and students debated the meaning of the texts they studied in an effort to get beyond their literal interpretation. To this very day, Jewish Torah study is referred to as chevruta, or study between two friends/partners, and is more like a debate. After all, both study partners come to a text with two different backgrounds, personalities and life history from which to interpret meaning buried below the surface of the literal text. Regarding text study and the desire to go beneath the literal translation, participants will learn how Jews approach biblical study (e.g., literal first, then the more important symbolic, allegoric and mystical layers of interpreting texts – and of course, debate).  Participants in the conversation can apply these methods to the study of their own texts.  Going beyond the literal interpretation offers great promise to a constructive interfaith dialogue.

Judaism also offers to interfaith dialogue and community-building the concept of "*shalom*," or peace. The word shalom is related to the word "*shalem*," wholeness, and suggests that peace – internal and external – comes from striving for and maintaining integrity, balance, completeness. A related Jewish concept is the Jewish mystical belief known as *"tikkun olam,"* which can be interpreted as repairing the world (of Divinity). *Tikkun olam* sees every person as a participant in the healing of the broken world. Derived from a central myth of Jewish mystical teachings, the act of repair relates to humanity's continuous quest to fit together the number of shards of Divine Light that spread across the Universe at the moment of Creation.[41] For Jews, every fulfilled commandment and every act of loving kindness redeems these shards of scattered Divine Light, bringing us all ever closer to higher levels of consciousness and the Divine Presence.[42] I say this brings us closer to the messianic age of peace and tranquility, as we come together as One.

Finally, I believe that G-d also knows that human beings process things differently, and therefore, there is a variety of spiritual beliefs that all lead to the same experience – oneness with Divinity. Think of a tall mountain. There are several paths that one can climb toward the top; however, all pathways lead to the same place – the summit – and the summit points up toward the Heavens. This example implies that perhaps G-d, or whatever any religion refers to as a godhead or Divine entity (or entities), knew that humankind needed different pathways to communicate with, process, experience or perceive a Higher Power. We are all connected by a loving energy within. Judaism offers one possible pathway toward the Source of that loving energy within and does not deny or reject the pathways that others travel toward the top of the mountain.

Jewish theology varies across the spectrum, and believers in other religions will likely find some aspect of Jewish theology to which they will resonate and see the similarities to their own practice and beliefs. They may also witness the power of debate and the ability to remain in community, while sharing fiercely different opinions, all the while respecting the other's point of view.

Judaism offers a lot to other religions, from an all-powerful G-d who exerts Divine Justice, to a merciful and loving G-d who is endlessly patient and expects nothing more than imperfect humans who at least try their best to do the right thing. From rote prayers to meditation and chanting, others will see similarities in Jewish ritual and observance. The biblical prophet Zechariah said in chapter 14, verse 9: "...and G-d shall be Sovereign over all the Earth; in that day there shall be one G-d with One name." Many progressive Jewish prayerbooks interpret this text as, "...and on that day, G-d's name shall be One and we all shall be One." Since I believe that Zechariah spoke from the One Source, I believe that he confirms my underlying notion about interfaith engagement: We all follow different paths up the mountain to the summit, and the summit always points to One place – Heaven.

# Notes

1. Philip Birnbaum, *Encyclopedia of Jewish Concepts* (New York: Hebrew Publishing Company, 1998), p. 81.
2. Harold S. Kushner, *To Life!* (New York: Warner Books, 1993), pp. 20-21.
3. Birnbaum, pp. 550-551.
4. Joseph Telushkin, *Jewish Literacy* (New York: HarperCollins, 1991), p. 27.
5. Ibid., p. 105.
6. Birnbaum, p. 60.
7. Ibid., p. 328.
8. Ibid., p. 630.
9. Wayne Dosick, *Living Judaism* (San Francisco: HarperCollins, 1995), p. 214.
10. Birnbaum, p. 429.
11. Ibid., p. 206.
12. Kushner, p. 201.
13. Ammiel Hirsch, "Our Literary Legacy," *Keeping Posted*, Vol. XXXIII, No. 3, p. 15.
14. Birnbaum, p. 345.
15. Telushkin, p. 149.
16. Birnbaum, p. 244.
17. George Robinson, *Essential Judaism* (New York: Pocket Books, 2000), p. 24.
18. Telushkin, p. 725.
19. Dosick, p. 128.
20. Birnbaum, p. 153.
21. Anita Diamant, *Living a Jewish Life* (New York: HarperCollins, 2007), pp. 54-57.
22. Eli Barnavi, *A Historical Atlas of the Jewish People* (New York: Schoken Books, 2002), p. 44.
23. Ibid., p. 4.
24. Dosick, p. 167.
25. Kushner, p. 155.
26. Harold Kushner, *When Bad Things Happen to Good People* (New York: Avon Books, 1980), p. 59.
27. Simcha Paull Raphael, *Jewish Views of the Afterlife* (Northvale, NJ: Jason Aronson, Inc., 1996), p. 145.
28. David A. Cooper, *God is a Verb* (New York: Berkley Publishing Group, 1997), p. 262.
29. Raphael, p. 144.
30. Cooper, p. 273.

31. Ibid., p. 291.

32. Raphael, p. 318.

33. Dr. Byron Sherwin, "Jewish Mysticism," Lecture Series, Spertus Institute of Jewish Studies, Chicago, IL, 1995.

34. Dr. Byron Sherwin, *Kabbalah: An Introduction to Jewish Mysticism* (Lanham, MD: Rowman & Littfield Publishers, Inc., 2006), p. 150.

35. Robinson, p. 224.

36. Sherwin, p. 119.

37. Ibid., p. 231.

38. Telushkin, p. 432.

39. Ibid., p. 459.

40. Ibid., p. 460.

41. Sherwin, p. 106.

42. Cooper, p. 179.

# Glossary

**BCE** – Before the Common Era; aligns with the Christian use of before Christ [BC]

**CE** – Common Era; aligns with the Christian use of the Latin phrase anno Domini, "in the year of our Lord"

**Cantor** – Ordained leader for Jewish sacred music or chanting

**Challah** – Traditional egg bread that is braided and eaten on Sabbath and holidays, except for Passover

**Chevruta** – From the Hebrew root word for friend; engaging in a dialogue by studying biblical texts with a partner

**Chanukiah** – The eight-stemmed menorah, with a ninth "helper" candle used on the holiday called Chanukah; the ninth "helper candle" is used to light a candle for each night and progresses until all eight candles are lit on the eighth evening

**Chavurah** – A small, Jewish spiritual community, similar to what Christians refer to as fellowship groups for Bible study

**Conservative Judaism** – A movement between Reform and Orthodox, it adheres to and obeys Jewish law, yet makes room for modern applications of Jewish law according to societal changes.

**Diaspora** – Refers to Jews scattered throughout the world away from the land of Israel; centered in Jerusalem; began with the Babylonian destruction of the First Temple and exile in 586 BCE; further extended by the destruction of the Second Temple and exile by the Romans in 70 CE.

**Elijah's Cup** – A fifth cup of wine placed on the Passover Seder table for a post-meal ritual. The Prophet Elijah represents the future Jewish redemption and coming of the Messianic Age

**Eternal Light** – As defined in Exodus 27:20, an olive oil lamp to burn in the Tabernacle; modern use is a light always lit and hanging above or standing next to the Holy Ark of a synagogue

**Gehenna/Gehinnom** – Similar to the Catholic "Purgatory," it is a place where the soul travels upon separating from the body at the time of death and, according to tradition, stays for up to 12 months for purgation and purification before moving on to the *Gan Eden* (Garden of Eden, or Paradise, or Heaven).

**Hebrew Bible** – Acronymn is TaNaCh, and is comprised of the books of Torah, Nevi'im (Prophets) and Ketuvim (Writings)

**Holy Ark** – The structure at the front of the synagogue sanctuary that houses the Torah (or several Torahs); resembles the portable tabernacle used to carry the Pact of the Covenant (some refer to as the 10 Commandments or The Teaching) during the 40-year wandering in the Wilderness and eventually placed in the First Temple in Jerusalem

**Israel** – The Torah recounts how Jacob's name was changed (Genesis 32) to Israel, "one who wrestles with G-d." Also refers to the modern state of Israel.

**Jewish population** – The current Jewish population in the entire world is about 13.5 million, of which about 8 million live in the Diaspora. About 6 million Jews live in the United States and Canada.

**Kiddush** – a sanctification prayer, as in the prayer for wine on Sabbath. The Hebrew root means "to make holy."

**Kiddush cup** – wine cup used to make Kiddush on Sabbath

**Kippah/kippot** (plural) – Skullcap (*Yarmulke* in Yiddish) worn by men (Orthodox men wear a kippah at all waking moments) as a sign of respect to G-d. In the progressive movements, men and some women wear kippot during religious services, rituals or celebrations.

**Matzah** – Unleavened bread eaten ritually on Passover

**Menorah** – Per Exodus 25:31-40, the seven-stem olive oil lamp of gold was used in the portable Tabernacle set up by Moses in the wilderness and later in the Temple in Jerusalem. The menorah has been a symbol of Judaism since biblical times and is the emblem on the coat of arms of the state of Israel. An eight-stem menorah (Chanukiah) is used to celebrate the holiday of Chanukah.

**Mezuzah** – Encases a scroll containing the text of Deuteronomy 6:4-9 and 11:18-21, with the first text being: "Hear, O Israel, the Eternal our God, the Eternal is One." The mezuzah is affixed at least two-thirds of the way up the right doorpost, with the top part leaning in to the inside of the structure. The mezuzah is a touchstone to remind Jews of their spiritual obligations; similar in function to a *tallit* (see).

**Midrash** – From the root "to search out," midrash is a method of drawing out deeper meaning from biblical texts. Some midrashim (plural) are stories, some are discourses, and some are allegorical references to fill gaps or discover underlying principles.

**Mikveh** – The ritual bath used for spiritual immersion and rebirth. Orthodox and some Conservative women use the mikveh monthly as part of the marital purity rituals. Some men and women immerse before major holidays or Sabbath. Mikveh immersion is also required for conversion to Judaism.

**Minyan** – A minimum of 10 adult Jews (males only in the Orthodox tradition); Jewish adults are older than 13 years of age (12 years of age for girls).

**Mitzvah** – Singular word for commandment. Mitzvot is the plural. Not all mitzvot are good deeds, such as observing the Sabbath or fasting on Yom Kippur. However, good deeds are almost always mitzvot. Of the 613 mitzvot identified in the Torah, approximately half are not relevant, because they pertain to rituals and practices related to the Temple sacrificial cult and maintenance (including agricultural tithes to the Priests)

**Niggun** – A mystical, musical prayer without words, typically focusing on repetitive sound, such as "la," " bim/bam," or "doi, doi, doi"

**Orthodox Judaism** – the most fundamental approach to Jewish practice, where the Divinely given Torah is not influenced by man's interpretation, and strict observance of Jewish law takes precedence over modernity

**Reconstructionist Judaism** – A movement inspired by Mordechai Kaplan, it sees the power of the Divine within all of man and Judaism as an ongoing and dynamic "religious civilization"; focuses on communal gathering for prayer, culture and learning

**Reform Judaism** – The most progressive of the Jewish movements, it adheres to modern interpretations of Jewish law, where such interpretation does not conflict with the basic beliefs of Judaism. There is a strong emphasis on the ethical commandments and social action.

**Sabbath** – The Jewish Sabbath, from sunset on Friday through just after sunset on Saturday. The Talmud defines 39 prohibited acts of work on the Day of Rest; worship includes the study of Torah and related texts of the Prophets.

**Sabbath seder** – The rituals of bringing in the Sabbath: lighting Sabbath candles, blessing/sanctifying a cup of wine, blessing children and blessing the Challah.

**Siddur** – Jewish prayer book that contains prayers according to a liturgical structure for daily, Sabbath and festival services. Along with the Torah and Talmud, the Siddur is a very important text for Jews

**Synagogue** – the place where Jews come together to pray, congregate and study. Synagogues probably came into existence after the destruction of the Temple in Jerusalem and the ensuing Babylonian exile in 586 BCE.

**Tabernacle** – See Holy Ark

**Tallit** – (Refers to Numbers 15:37-40) Prayer shawl worn during daylight prayer with fringes on the four corners; the fringes remind the worshipper of the commandments (mitzvot)

**Talmud** – While the Torah is considered the Written Law, tradition states that the Oral Law was passed down from generation to generation beginning with Moses at Sinai. The Oral Law was first written as the Mishneh ("to repeat") in 200 CE. The Gemara ("completion") was new commentary on the Mishneh and was written in approximately 500 CE. The Talmud is referred to as the Gemara for some and both the Mishneh and Gemara for others. The Talmud is a record of rabbinic discussions pertaining to Jewish law, ethics, philosophy, customs and history.

**Torah** – The term refers to "guidance and instruction" and is comprised of the five books of Moses: Genesis, Exodus, Leviticus, Numbers and Deuteronomy. The Torah makes up the first five books of the Hebrew Bible.

**Tzitzit** – Fringes on the corners of a tallit that are comprised of eight strings wrapped (7, 8, 11 and 13 wraps) and knotted (five knots between each set of wraps). Tzitzit are a reminder of the 613 commandments (mitzvot) and the phrase, "The Eternal is One"

**Yom Kippur** – also called the Day of Atonement; one of the High Holy Days

ඥ

## For Further Reading

Barnavi, Eli. *A Historical Atlas of the Jewish People*. New York: Schocken Books, 1992.

Birnbaum, Philip. *Encyclopedia of Jewish Concepts*. New York: Hebrew Publishing Company, 1998.

Cooper, David A. *God is a Verb*. New York: Riverhead Books, 1997.

Diamant, Anita. *Living a Jewish Life*. New York: HarperCollins Publishers, 2007.

Dosick, Wayne. *Living Judaism*. CA: HarperCollins Publishers, 1997.

Editors. JPS Hebrew-English Tanach. PA: The Jewish Publication Society, 1999.

Hirsch, Ammiel. "Our Literacy Legacy," Keeping Posted, Vol. XXXIII, No. 3, 1995.

Kushner, Harold S. *When Bad Things Happen to Good People*. New York: Avon Books, 1981.

Kushner, Harold S. *To Life!*, New York: Warner Books, 1993.

Raphael, Simcha Paull. *Jewish Views of the Afterlife*. NJ: Jason Aronson, Inc., 1996.

Robinson, George. *Essential Judaism*. NewYork: Pocket Books, 2000.

Sherwin, Dr. Byron L. *Kabbalah: An Introduction to Jewish Mysticism*. MD: Rowman & Littlefield, Inc., 2006.

Sherwin, Dr. Byron L. "Jewish Mysticism," Lecture series, Spertus Institute of Jewish Studies, Chicago, IL, 1995.

Telushkin, Joseph. *Jewish Literacy*. New York: HarperCollins Publishers, Inc., 1991.

*Christian Sacred Space*

CHAPTER TWO

*The Church: Sacred Space of Christians*

*Tom Buchanan*

### Welcome to the church!

It is my intention to set out the meaning of the church and to describe to an outsider what each aspect of the sacred space means to a Christian. I will explore how the different symbols in this space fit into the Christian's faith, worship and life. What is the Church? This simple question evokes numerous images and answers. Some responses might be that the church is . . .

* A building dedicated to the worship of God.
* A gathering place for Christians.
* A school for learning about Jesus and his will for us.
* A Catholic, Orthodox, Protestant, conservative or liberal place for Christian worship.
* A denomination like Methodist, Baptist, Pentecostal or Presbyterian.
* The Body of Christ
* The Fellowship of Believers

The definition of "Church" will mean that most churches will describe their sacred space slightly differently, but the description that I will give of the sacred space of Christians is similar in all churches. Catholic space might be more formal with statues of saints, which a Protestant church will not have. A liturgical Protestant church will be different in style and form from an independent or mega-church. Since I am Protestant and because I know more about Protestant churches, I will describe a typical Protestant church with its sacred space.

## Every Space Tells a Story

Over the last several years, I have come to be quite a fan of TV shows involving interior design and home improvement. Growing up, I was always an analytical type, more interested in equations and facts than colors and aesthetics, but people do change. Over time, through both my evolving taste in TV shows and my increasing willingness to broaden my experience, I have become more and more aware of how the spaces in our homes, schools and offices represent more than a mere collection of "stuff." These particular spaces are also a vehicle for expressing some truth or meaning. They bespeak a form of reality.

*Every space tells a story.* Choice of colors ... selection and placement of furniture ... design for use of the space ... all come together and, if successful, please the eye and satisfy the mind. But, taken together, they do more. They communicate something about those who use the room ... who they are ... what they care about ... perhaps even what they hope for. Hence, on one level, a space may appear to be quite ordinary and devoid of meaning. However, on another, it can be a window to the sacred dimension of human experience. I know of many such places – places where the very human and the very divine seem to merge into a magnificent fusion of beauty and meaning.

For me, one of those places was my childhood church, a Presbyterian church – rooted in the Reformed tradition of Protestant Christianity. From one perspective there was nothing particularly special about it. It looked like most other churches I knew. But inside, with a child's open mind and heart, it was a place where I was certain God lived, where angels walked and where my heroes worshipped. Almost everything in it – its stained glass, the dimensions of its worship space, the arrangement of its furnishings, its symbols – reinforced my childlike perceptions of God. Today in the hurried pace of this world if I should return to that childhood church, it would immediately take me back to a place where I was first touched with the Mystery of God. Making that journey would resurrect the memory of those primary days where my life was first touched by the Mystery and my heart would be lifted and strengthened. I have also known other churches like that ... without the weight of nostalgia to be sure, but nevertheless, places with spaces that tell a story and invite all who enter into that story and the life-giving experiences that story can bestow. Allow me to invite you into such a space – the sort of space which over time I have come to regard as home and where its compelling story is regularly told.

The place to which I invite you is not every church; rather, it is a typical church in the Reformed and Protestant tradition in which I was reared and in which I have practiced my faith for over forty years. As you arrive, you may see two or more buildings making up the campus. Often, one building stands out, if for no other reason than it has a steeple with a high Cross rising over it pointing toward heaven. This cross-symbol marks the Sanctuary, the principal worship space of the congregation. Often next to this Sanctuary stands another smaller building, usually a multi-purpose structure with fellowship space, classrooms, and administrative offices. The two buildings are often connected by an outside walkway or by a connecting hallway. In most cases with which I am familiar, the principal entrance for congregants and visitors is through this latter building. Walk inside and you will enter or be very near a public gathering area, and it may appear fairly ordinary. But to the imaginative eye, something else lurks there.

There is more because the place – the space – tells a story. Every part of the space in this building contributes to the story, even if it takes imagination to discern it. This is a story that Christians have been telling ever since some fishermen on the Sea of Galilee dropped their nets and followed an itinerant carpenter-turned-preacher from Nazareth more than 2000 years ago.

So, welcome! Look around! Permit me to point out some things that are important to notice in the space where an old, old story is regularly told.

## The Public Gathering Space

We are now in what some churches call an Atrium, others a Fellowship Hall. Whatever it is called, it is a place for people to gather prior to entering the Sanctuary. Looking around and taking it all in, you might think that the space doesn't look very "religious," and *you would be absolutely right*. It appears pretty ordinary: perhaps an information kiosk with brochures and pamphlets ... perhaps an American flag to remind you of our freedom to worship ... perhaps a large table with more flyers and with name tags and markers so that others can get to know your name and you can identify other worshipers. In this space you generally will not see a cross or a painting of Jesus or hear Christian music playing, all of which would tell you that you are in a public gathering area. Little here suggests the mysteries that lie beyond.

But *every* space tells a story, even a space with few religious symbols. The room's non-religious feel is not accidental. The worldly air of the room is itself the message! It was in the world that the Christian faith was born, and it is in the world that it is lived and brought to maturity. You need only to recall that

Jesus was born in a manger and crucified on a cross on a hill outside the city of Jerusalem to see the worldly side of the Christian faith. There is no "private" Christianity. As the twentieth-century Lutheran theologian Dietrich Bonhoeffer (1906-1945) wrote:

*I discovered later, and I'm still discovering right up to this moment, that it is only by living completely in this world that one learns to have faith ... By this worldliness I mean living unreservedly in life's duties, problems, successes and failures, experiences and perplexities. In so doing we throw ourselves completely into the arms of God, taking seriously, not our own sufferings, but those of God in the world – watching with Christ in Gethsemane.*[1]

Christian faith is seen so often as a "private" matter from the point-of-view of a twenty-first century person. Truly Christian sensibilities must embrace the whole of *public* life – the private and the public come together in the wholeness of God's embrace. We share this life with others, with friends and neighbors of all paths and persuasions, and in this space we look forward to meeting them, talking with them and catching up on their lives. The easy access communicates openness and hospitality to all who walk through the doors. Here, we find joy in the activities, advertised with flyers and brochures, which call us together and which help us to develop tighter bonds of community. We feel a common pride in our country, often symbolized by the presence of our national flag, evoking gratitude for those who have sacrificed that we might gather freely. And we somehow know that whatever lies beyond this space can help us live better lives and be better people.

### Transition

Leaving the public gathering space, we walk outside, or often, we enter a hallway or an even smaller space which is clearly meant as a transition between the casual atmosphere of the gathering space and the more formal air of the room beyond. Look around and you may notice closets ... or corners stacked with supplies ... or sacred art. There are often no chairs and the space is usually too small for us to tarry very long. To provide lingering space, of course, is not its purpose. The dimensions of this space and furnishings in it point beyond toward a mystery that entices all who enter. And yet, we sense there is a reason that we are not immediately walking into the worship space itself.

Perhaps we are reminded that what lies beyond those doors is a very special place, the sort of place that demands our full attention. The room, so apparently pointless at first, gives us a chance to transition, to adjust to what is being asked of us, that we might enter what lies beyond with the senses prepared, that we might bring with us, as expressed in Wordsworth's memorable phrase, "a heart that watches and receives."[2] The open doors beckon us to do just that – enter, watch, receive.

## In the Sanctuary

As we open the doors and walk in, we may be thrown off-balance or at least have to catch our breath as we enter this mammoth space. The space before, so small and constricted, suddenly opens up, giving way to a large expanse of space and multiple visual images, evocative of the majesty and grandeur of God. Every church I have ever visited – no matter how large or small, whether prosperous or poor – has had this effect on me. The principal worship space is very special. Consecrated by the prayers and praises, the songs and the tears, which have been offered within the walls, a Sanctuary draws wonder and worship out of even the hardest heart. Drawn by a strange but gracious magnetism, many have been lifted up out of themselves, have been called indeed to *forget themselves*, and to join with hundreds of others in the worship of the living God. In the words of Fanny Crosby's great hymn, "This is my story, this is my song, praising my Savior all the day long!"

The cross up front dominates the sanctuary. Not a person can miss this symbol which looms large over all else in the space. It is clearly the focal point of the room. And with it, indeed this entire space has a story. The sacred symbol of the cross is ubiquitous, as likely to be seen as a piece of jewelry in a rock star's ears or in a business logo as at the front of a church sanctuary. But two thousand years ago, it was not a symbol to wear, so much as *something that could wear you* – should you be so unfortunate as to offend the Roman imperial state in one of its many provinces. Punishment was often crucifixion on a cross. This, of course, was the experience of Jesus, the humble carpenter-turned-itinerant preacher, with a certain knack for addressing the failures of the people and strongly inviting them to repent and follow his example.

Condemned as an enemy of the state for his revolutionary teaching of the Kingdom of God, Jesus suffered a humiliating, public death; he was nailed and tied to a cross. His followers and friends largely abandoned him. After he was buried in a cave-tomb later on the same day, the Roman authorities and their collaborators had good reason to suppose that his movement, his memory and his deeds would be buried with him. We too might think that.

But we would be wrong.

Soon after his resurrection, his followers proclaimed his name and spoke of his deeds with a conviction that they would carry to their graves. Their Master was no longer dead, but he had been raised from death by God, vindicating his life and his message and giving to all who place their trust in him an assurance that no power of this world could overcome them. Not Rome, not hate, not bigotry, not fear, not even death itself was stronger than the self-giving, self-sacrificing love of God. This love manifested itself in God's boundless mercy, God's passion for forgiveness and God's desire to bless the world and make it new.

All of this belongs to what the Cross means for Christians. When they look at a cross, they see far more than two perpendicular pieces of wood. They see sacrifice. They see unfathomable love. And paradoxically, they see *life*. And this meaning which radiates from the cross invests this sacred space with a meaning that transforms minds and hearts of those who enter to worship. This transformation streams from a faith rooted in a sure and certain conviction of God's love and acceptance of all people everywhere.

But why a cross? Why not an open, empty tomb if the Resurrection is the great miracle of Christian faith?

The message of the cross is one that contradicts reason, or at least what ordinarily passes as reason. By any stretch of the imagination, the message is not an easy one to swallow. To many, the idea is simply foolish! When the preacher proclaims that people are "saved" by believing that the God who moves the sun and the other stars was acting, in love, through the grisly death of Jesus, it does not make sense. Alternately, the idea of God's saving people by the death of Jesus on the cross may even be offensive. How could a good and just God allow His Chosen One to endure such a death at the hands of sinners? And yet, the Christian witness has always been just that. The chief interpreter of Christ, the Apostle Paul, states in a letter to the church at Corinth:

*For the message of the cross is foolishness to those who are perishing, but to us who are being saved it is the power of God. For it is written: 'I will destroy the wisdom of the wise; the intelligence of the intelligent I will frustrate.' Where is the wise man? Where is the scholar? Where is the philosopher of this age? Has not God made foolish the wisdom of the world? For since in the wisdom of God, the world through its wisdom did not know him, God was pleased through the foolishness of what was preached to save those who believe.*

*Jews demand miraculous signs and Greeks look for wisdom, but we preach Christ crucified: a stumbling block to Jews and foolishness to Gentiles, but to those whom God has called, both Jews and Greeks, Christ the power of God and the wisdom of God. For the foolishness of God is wiser than man's wisdom, and the weakness of God is stronger than man's strength.*[3]

Although the cross is difficult, it is the heart of the Christian story and the Church's. Like any great symbol, it is subject to various interpretations. Some see in it a kind of debt that Jesus paid to God with his life to redeem broken and lost humanity from sin. Others see the cross as God's master act of tricking the Devil out of his claim on the human race. Still others see Jesus' willingness to experience and take upon himself the full depth of human pain and alienation, bearing them as an example of what God's love looks like as it beckons us to follow him into the world in ministry to all who suffer. Christians believe that Jesus' death on the cross is the basis of our reconciliation with God. We are made right with God, not by our own efforts, but through the gracious offer of forgiveness from the Creator. However one understands it, the Cross is not optional for the Christian. There is no Christianity without the Cross.

To say that it *should* be the focal point of the Sanctuary is a bit of an understatement. It, in fact, is the focal point of the Sanctuary because it is the center of the Christian faith, the ultimate sign of God's love for the whole world and the ultimate inspiration to all who seek to reach out to a suffering, dying world with a message of reconciliation and hope.

### Under the Cross

If the focal point of a Sanctuary is the Cross, then that which is under it and around it ought to be there to support and accentuate its message, the means by which the Christian story is told and enacted. One of these supports in any Sanctuary is the Pulpit, a raised speaking platform from which scripture is read and the message of God's love in the life, death, and resurrection of Jesus Christ is proclaimed. The Protestant tradition strongly emphasizes preaching from the text of scripture. A Sunday sermon normally is based upon a reading or readings from the Bible (Old or New Testament), and the preacher seeks to correlate the message of the text(s) with the context of the listeners today. The sermon seeks to convey the truth contained in the ancient writings in a way that their truth interacts with and transforms the lives of the listeners. The sermon seeks to address both those inside and outside the Christian community with a message of comfort, guidance, correction, and hope.

The Bible lies open on the pulpit. For Christians, the Bible contains the Word of God. The Scriptures are the supreme source of the teaching of the Church and also the source for the proclamation of the gospel. We believe that God spoke through the events, stories, parables, and sayings in the Bible and that God continues to speak through these words and events today. People come into the sanctuary Sunday after Sunday hoping to hear a word from God that will give direction and meaning to their lives. The multiplied times that God has spoken to individuals or to a whole community of people provides experiences of the holy that cannot be forgotten. These accumulated experiences of the holy make the space sacred. Christians do not worship the cross and neither do they worship the Bible, but these two symbols mediate to the worshippers a sense of God's presence. The strength of the Sacred depends upon the vividness of the memory of God's Voice being heard in the heart.

## The Sacraments

The Sacraments stand alongside the preaching of the Word of God, which are the Church's ways of *enacting* the written and spoken word of God. St. Augustine (354-430) famously defined a sacrament as "an outward sign of an invisible grace" – a physical, tangible act that demonstrates a deeper spiritual reality. The Roman Catholic Church recognizes seven sacraments: Baptism, Confirmation, Holy Communion, Confession, Marriage, Holy Orders, and the Anointing of the Sick. Churches born from the Protestant Reformation recognize only two: Baptism and the Lord's Supper. The latter is also known as "Communion" or the "Eucharist." These two acts, symbolized by a font and a table, take place under the cross as part of its meaning.

## The Font

The fonts which are found in many churches are intended for baptisms using a non-immersion method, such as sprinkling or pouring. A simple font has a pedestal about three and a half feet high with a holder for a basin of water. The materials used may vary greatly, like carved or sculpted marble, wood, or metal. The shape can vary. For example, some are three-sided as a reminder of the Christian doctrine of the Trinity: Father, Son, and Holy Spirit.

Fonts are often placed at or near the entrance to the sanctuary to remind believers of their baptism as they enter the church to worship, since the rite of baptism served as their initiation into the Church. But fonts may also be placed on the floor of the sanctuary or on a platform near the pulpit. In the church with which I am most familiar, the font is placed beside the pulpit, and weekly, before the confession of sin, water is poured from a pitcher into the basin, while the worshippers are encouraged to remember their baptism. Each week they are invited to recall that they were baptized into Christ's Body by the sprinkling of water on their heads (or their body immersed in water), the minister pronouncing God's blessing. The Sacrament of Baptism signifies God's claiming us as His own, God's cleansing us of all that separates us from Him, and of renewing us for a life dedicated to God's glory and love.

This sacrament is administered only *once* in a person's life. While different traditions in Christianity have different ideas of what happens in this sacrament and who is a proper recipient for it, the churches of the Reformation have always affirmed that baptism is for those who affirm belief in Jesus Christ as their Lord and Savior *and for their children, including infants.* While some question the practice of baptizing children and young people who cannot intelligently affirm faith in Christ for themselves, the majority of the world's Christians have always understood the baptism of young children as a radical statement of God's initiative in loving and claiming us before we can "do" anything to merit that love. [Later, as children baptized as infants mature, they go through the process called Confirmation, in which they study and personally appropriate the meaning of their baptism for their lives.]

Consider how the baptismal event sacralizes the space in which it is administered. First, believers are confident that God acts through our actions. When the official places the water of baptism on the head of the recipient, we believe that in a way that defies analysis, God is in this act revealing the forgiveness of sin in the person being baptized. The act of pouring water into the bowl in the font and saying the words of remembrance continue to call us back to our own initiation into the family of God. In addition to this aspect of baptism, members of the congregation also recall the day that they brought their children to the church requesting baptism and how the whole congregation agreed to help them rear their children in the "nurture and admonition of the Lord." With this understanding of baptism, it is no wonder that this space possesses a sacred quality.

## The Table

In the sanctuary of most churches on the level of the congregation sits a large wooden table. This table symbolizes the last supper that Jesus had with his disciples. And today it is a table to which we are invited to eat and drink with him. This table is called the "Lord's table" because it is an extension of the supper that he shared with his disciples so many years ago.

The supper Jesus observed was a Jewish Passover meal, but as Jesus shared this meal with his disciples before his suffering and death, he reinterpreted the Passover in light of his coming and offering of himself for the sins of whole world. Then he commanded his disciples to observe this supper after his death as a way of remembering him. This is the way the Apostle Paul describes how the institution was passed on to him:

For I received from the Lord what I also passed on to you: The Lord Jesus, on the night he was betrayed, took bread, and when he had given thanks, he broke it and said, "This is my body, which is for you; do this in remembrance of me." In the same way, after supper he took the cup, saying, "This cup is the new covenant in my blood; do this, whenever you drink it, in remembrance of me." For whenever you eat this bread and drink this cup, you proclaim the Lord's death until he comes.[4]

As with baptism, the Sacrament of the Lord's Supper is variously interpreted across Christian tradition. The interpretation ranges from communion being the vehicle by which the saving "Body" and "Blood" of Christ is literally received by the believer, to being a purely symbolic act, commemorating Christ's sacrifice. In the tradition begun by one the great Protestant reformers, John Calvin, it is understood as a communal act in which the Spirit of God brings worshippers into a spiritual communion with Christ, both re-enacting and confirming the spiritual reality of believers' union with Him. However it is understood, this supper points to the centrality of Christ's offering of himself for the life of the world. It points to an act of love which is not only to be believed, but also an act in which contemporary believers in Christ participate through their self-giving service to others.

If you are a Christian, imagine yourself sitting in the sanctuary with all the other baptized believers and with them receiving the Lord's body and blood. The communion ritual rehearses with gratitude the creation act, the revelation of God's love through the ages, and the remembrance of the Last Supper of Christ with his disciples. Like those disciples of old, we find ourselves at the table;

Christ is our host; his presence is with us and in us. Every communion is a time of "beginning again," a new start in life with the assurance that we are forgiven and accepted by God. Again this enactment deepens the sense of the sacred in us and in the space where it occurs.

## The Choir

In most churches there is one other thing that catches the eye and which might be missed because of the force of the other symbols which fill the space. I am referring to the presence of from a dozen to fifty chairs sitting in rows beneath the cross. In most worship services, a choir occupies these seats and fills this sacred space with words and music. Christians celebrate the Word of God not only in speech, but also with song; the Christian gospel is celebrated and shared in music. Between leading the people in singing hymns and lifting up hearts through musical testimony to the glory of God, the choir adds an essential element to Christian worship.  Worship is not only spoken words and enacted rituals; it also includes the feelings and insights communicated through music. When I was a very young child, I had quite an exalted view of choir members. As they processed into the sanctuary at the beginning of worship, I imagined that they were angels! While it is true that I've never known a choir member to sprout wings, perhaps I was more right than not. Whether located up front or in the rear of the sanctuary, a dedicated choir ministers to the people as surely as any clergy.  Both clergy and choir members share the Word of God and celebrate not only with spoken witness, but also through the word which is sung and shared in music:

*When in our music God is glorified,*
*And adoration leaves no room for pride,*
*It is as though the whole creation cried:*
*Alleluia!*

*How often, making music, we have found*
*A new dimension in the world of sound,*
*As worship moved us to a more profound*
*Alleluia!* [5]

## The Worship of God's People

We have pointed out all the furnishings of the sanctuary of a church. Knowing the names of the pieces of furniture without knowing how all of these serve the Christian week after week is something like knowing the names of the instruments in an orchestra without having heard them being played. Every Sunday, and also at other times of worship, the various elements in the sanctuary are used to create the experience of worshiping God.

Worship on Sunday brings together members of the church to hear the word of God read and proclaimed and to join in singing hymns that offer worship to God. They pray, listen, commit themselves to God and find in the service of worship consolation, guidance and hope. The people "gather in God's name," they receive God's Word, they give thanks to God and they are sent out into the world to serve. All of this is clearly set forth in a printed bulletin entitled "Service for the Lord's Day."

Here is a typical bulletin of a worship service in a Reformed church. First, read through this Order of Worship, and then notice how each movement contributes to the worship of God.

### Service for the Lord's Day

*5th Sunday in Ordinary Time*

### WE GATHER IN GOD'S NAME

**†PRELUDE**
**†WELCOME AND ANNOUNCEMENTS**
**CHORAL INTROIT** *Cantad!*
Chapel Choir
- Sing to the Lord a new song. Come and lift up a song to the Lord.
  - Sing a song of gladness, O people, lift your voice.
  - Sing to God a new song, Let all the earth rejoice.

**\*CALL TO WORSHIP**
Leader: Praise the Lord, O my soul!
People: I will praise the Lord as long as I live.
Leader: Blessed are those whose hope is in the Lord their God, who keeps faith forever.

People: The Lord lifts up those who are bowed down. The Lord watches over the stranger.

Leader: The Lord God will reign forever. Let our worship begin!

**\*OPENING HYMN** No. 420 *God of Grace and God of Glory*

**\*CALL TO CONFESSION**

**\*PRAYER OF CONFESSION**

*Lord God, forgive our feeble efforts to make you over to fit our image.*

*It is easier to restate your truth in easy clichés than it is to speak in words that change minds.*

*It is easier to rewrite your hope in easy answers than it is to see through perplexity.*

*It is easier to rethink your grace in easy pardon than it is to modify our ways.*

*By your Spirit, visit us with the full depth of your forgiveness and make us over to fit your image. We pray in the name of Jesus Christ. Amen.*

**\*KYRIE** Lord, have mercy upon us. Christ, have mercy upon us. Lord, have mercy upon us.

**\*ASSURANCE OF PARDON**

Leader: ...in Jesus Christ, we are forgiven.

People: Thanks be to God.

**†\*GLORIA PATRI**

Glory be to the Father,

and to the Son, and to the Holy Ghost;

As it was in the beginning, is now and ever shall be,

World without end. Amen, amen.

**TIME WITH CHILDREN**

*Following the Time With Children, children ages 3–kindergarten are invited to attend Cherub Choir in the Joyful Noise Room (3rd floor, Education building)*

WE RECEIVE GOD'S WORD

**SCRIPTURE READING** Isaiah 58:1-9a

Leader: This is the word of the Lord.

People: Thanks be to God!

**ANTHEM** *Tunaomba Mungu Atawele* -J. Paradowski

Chapel Choir

We pray God to reign.
We pray Jesus to reign.
We pray the Spirit to reign.

**SERMON:** *WHAT WORSHIP DOES* Rev. Christopher A. Henry

**\*HYMN** *We Are Called*
verse 1 – Choir --verses 2 and 3 - Congregation

## \*AFFIRMATION OF FAITH
I believe in God, the Father almighty,
Creator of Heaven and Earth.
I believe in Jesus Christ,
His only Son, our Lord.
He was conceived by the power of the Holy Spirit
and born of the Virgin Mary.
He suffered under Pontius Pilate,
was crucified, died, and was buried.
He descended to the dead.
On the third day he rose again.
He ascended into Heaven,
and is seated at the right hand of the Father.
He will come again to judge the living and the dead.
I believe in the Holy Spirit,
the holy catholic Church,
the communion of saints,
the forgiveness of sins,
the resurrection of the body,
and the life everlasting.
Amen.

## PASTORAL PRAYER AND THE LORD'S PRAYER
Our Father, who art in Heaven, hallowed be thy name. Thy kingdom come, thy will be done, on earth as it is in heaven. Give us this day our daily bread; and forgive us our debts, as we forgive our debtors; and lead us not into temptation, but deliver us from evil. For thine is the kingdom, and the power and the glory, forever. Amen.

## WE GIVE THANKS TO GOD

**OFFERTORY** *Silence the Stones* -C. Courtney
Chancel Choir, Resident Orchestra
**\*DOXOLOGY**
Praise God from whom all blessings flow,
Praise him all creatures here below,
Praise him above ye heavenly host,
Praise Father, Son, and Holy Ghost. Amen.
**\*PRAYER OF DEDICATION**

## WE ARE SENT TO SERVE

**\*HYMN** No. 411 *Arise, Your Light Is Come!*
**\*CHARGE AND BENEDICTION**
**\*CHORAL RESPONSE** Song of Hope
**POSTLUDE** *Bourrée in F Major* -G. Telemann

## EXPLANATION OF THE SERVICE FOR THE LORD'S DAY

### WE GATHER IN GOD'S NAME
We gather together as a people by entering the sanctuary quietly, finding
a seat and getting our hearts prepared to worship God. A musical prelude speaks
in a language beyond words to our hearts inviting us to worship God. A warm
welcome is extended to all, and the choir sings a short piece inviting us to "Sing
to the Lord a new song." The person leading worship (generally one of the
ministers) invites the congregation to engage in the worship of God by leading
the "Call to Worship" in which the leader speaks a line and the people respond.
(These parts are noted in the bulletin in dark and light-face type.)
The gathering for worship also includes a "Call to Confession," during
which time the congregation in unison confesses their sins to God. Sometimes
this is preceded by a time of silence to confess one's personal sins. Following
the confession the congregation asks God for mercy by singing the Kyrie – "Lord,
have mercy upon me...." The minister then offers the Assurance of Pardon,
declaring that God forgives our sins, to which the congregation responds by
saying, "Thanks be to God." Then the worshipers join together singing "Glory be

to the Father and to the Son and to the Holy Ghost." A short time of worship with the children follows.

## WE RECEIVE GOD'S WORD

The passage of scripture which serves as the basis for the sermon is generally read by the minister. Following the reading, the minister announces that this is "the word of the Lord" to which the people respond, "Thanks be to God!" The choir's anthem generally reflects the same theme as the scripture and the sermon.

The sermon offers the minister the opportunity to teach, using the richness of the Old and New Testaments, to proclaim the Good News of God's love, and to challenge listeners to live out their faith in their daily lives.

Following the sermon the congregation sings a hymn that expands the theme of the sermon. We should remember that music sometimes communicates in a manner that speaking cannot. In response to the sermon, the congregation together states what they believe. In many churches this is a recitation of the Apostle's Creed, an ancient confession which summarizes the Christian faith. During the pastoral prayer, the minister brings before God the concerns of the whole community of believers, including prayers of praise, thanksgiving and intercession. The congregation joins in praying the Lord's Prayer, the prayer that Jesus taught his disciples.

## WE GIVE THANKS TO GOD

The offering of thanks to God begins with music and continues as the morning offering is being received. Since the offering of money is an expression of the self, symbolically worshipers are offering their lives to God when they place a financial offering in the plate as it is passed. When the ushers have finished taking the offering, they place the gifts on the communion table as the congregation stands and sings "Praise God from whom all blessings flow...." With a prayer these gifts are dedicated to God, and the sanctuary is truly filled with gratitude for God's goodness and mercy.

## WE ARE SENT TO SERVE

The sending begins with a hymn that reinforces the sermon and draws to a conclusion the worship event. The minister charges the congregation to live as Christ's people in the world and prays a benediction (blessing) that they may have God's help in living out the truth they have received in this worship experience. The choir sings a brief response and the service of worship ends in the sanctuary but flavors life throughout the week.

## Out Among the People

The strong focus on the front of the sanctuary is both necessary and appropriate, but there is one remaining feature which usually dominates the room and must not be omitted. Thus far we have looked at this sacred space from the rear of the church forward, but if we walked to the front of the room and turned around, we would see another essential component of worship. If we had been studying the room from its middle, looking up front, we would have been standing among them the whole time ... *the pews*. While certainly leadership comes from the front, among the congregation of worshippers the most wonderful things happen. The Word is *heard* and *received*. The Word is *enacted* and calls for *participation*. The Word is *sung* and *celebrated* in music. Lives are touched and empowered, imbued with the energy of God's Spirit, and in this empowerment, the congregation is brought back to what it is – the "Body of Christ" in the world. Perhaps even the arrangement of the pews can be understood on a deeper level, as a sign of how worshippers are truly connected, one to another, in this Body.

The "Body of Christ"! This designation could mean just a group of people dedicated to Christ's way, doing his will in the world. But in the New Testament and particularly in the letters of the Apostle Paul, it speaks of mystery and wonder. The "Body of Christ" describes a mystical reality, the spiritual presence of Christ in the world, acting through his "body," the Church. Corporately, the members of the Church literally *re-present* Christ to the world and to each other. In the words of a poem written by the Spanish mystic Teresa of Avila (1515-1582):

Christ has no body but yours,
No hands, no feet on earth but yours,
Yours are the eyes with which he looks
Compassion on this world,
Yours are the feet with which he walks to do good,
Yours are the hands, with which he blesses all the world.
Yours are the hands, yours are the feet,
Yours are the eyes, you are his body.
Christ has no body now but yours,

No hands, no feet on earth but yours,
Yours are the eyes with which he looks
compassion on this world.
Christ has no body now on earth but yours.[6]

Unfortunately, most Christians don't habitually understand their life together in quite so profound a way. Theirs are ordinary lives of love and caring, of mentoring, worshipping, and sharing, but through their lives they embody the spiritual reality of the Christ whom they seek to follow in ways they can hardly imagine. Thus, they gather together with others who week after week come to meet Christ in such a space as we have explored. Regularly, they meet to feel the love and empowerment of God in their lives.

## Beyond the Building: Living Faithfully in the World

Indeed, every space tells a story. Through a visit to a church we have found a remarkable and powerful witness to the Christian story – the story of Jesus, the story of his life, his Cross, his Resurrection. We have been exposed to the various ways in which that story is proclaimed, preached, read, spoken, enacted, sung, and celebrated. As we leave this sacred space and go back out into the public gathering space, we have come full circle. We have returned to our starting point. And that's the point. The worship of God is both an end in itself as well as a preparation for lives of faithfulness with and towards others in the world.

Faithfulness calls church members to reach out to their neighbors. In times past, our neighbors tended to look like us and to believe like us. Today, we find that the cultural framework has changed radically. Christians have often known those of the Jewish faith as neighbors, and efforts at fellowship have had mixed results. But Muslims, Hindus, and Buddhists also are growing in numbers in many of our communities. These people of different colors and different religions are no longer just on the other side of the world, but rather the people on the other side of the street, and next door, and in an adjacent cubicle at work or the next desk at school. We buy from them. We sell to them. We work with them and have coffee with them. Our children marry them! Whether we desire it or not, pluralism is a reality. Today in most of our cities there are many beliefs, many ways of life, an assortment of values and cultural practices, but in all these "neighbors" there are those whose basic goodness and humanity we cannot deny simply because they are not like us.

Multiculturalism is spreading across the globe. Before the dawn of the twentieth century, it was most likely that we would likely live our entire life in more or less the same place, locked into a culture that knew next to nothing about other ways of being and living. If we were, for example, Japanese, our wisdom would be that of our village elders, who had learned their wisdom from their elders. We would speak Japanese. We would think in Japanese. We would see things in a peculiarly Japanese way. We would marry a Japanese spouse. Shintoism or Buddhism would likely have been our religion. And our own particular village – with its own even more specific customs – would probably be forever our whole world and our whole life.

Beginning in the latter half of the twentieth century and now at a blindingly accelerated rate, we have been moving into a new, wholly unprecedented phase of world history in which the barriers between previously unacquainted cultures are crumbling. All the world's diverse cultures, religions, customs, and rituals are available to us with the emergence of an ultra-connected, interdependent world.[7] Continued ignorance of other ways of life may offer temporary bliss, but it is increasingly difficult to maintain a closed mind, though it seems that some are doing their best to keep their eyes closed. But with the advent of world travel, the miracle of mass communications, and the Internet's promise of an open-book world only mouse clicks away, the move from the farming village to the global village, from tribal custom to an integral universal civilization seems increasingly to be both our destiny and our greatest moral challenge.

And a challenge it is. While it is increasingly difficult for thinking people to maintain the ethnocentric fiction that their own culture and beliefs are simply superior to all others, there are many who try to defend this idea. When people take this approach to others, the invocation of God's guarantee is often not far behind. It may be the god of "left-behind," end-time apocalyptic scenarios or the god who commands the beheading of civilian contractors. It may be the god of my one and only true church or the god of universal jihad. Religions and their institutions in these wonderfully promising, wildly dangerous times are far too often co-opted by those afraid of the future, afraid of a new order of dialogue and cooperation among communities and nations and peoples. What a beautiful world could be born if we could recognize our essential oneness as the creation of God! The vision of this higher and deeper reality would put to death the barrenness and darkness created by our egoism. What should serve as a vehicle for peace and justice has been captured by fear and pride and may result in the ultimate destruction of humanity. The challenge for those of us who are leaders in our respective religious communities is an intellectual and moral duty: to reclaim the name of God, of the Sacred, and honor that name by working together for that larger vision which makes sacred human life on this fragile planet.

Responding to this challenge will likely be a rough path. Being on the side of humanity offers no protection from the forces of division and destruction. Christianity has always taught that there is a Cross which stands between here and the Kingdom of God; to walk that path will demand perseverance in the face of conflict. Progress on the path will include suffering; it will call on men and women of courage and vision to confront "the blood-stained face history has taken on today. The grouping we need is a grouping... resolved to speak out clearly and pay up personally."[8]

For this speaking out and challenging the status quo, we must engage people of other faiths. If we are willing to drop our defenses and begin the process, a new world of faith, hope, and unity can be born. Interreligious dialogue is, therefore, a subversive act. It requires courage. It risks being misunderstood by one's own faith community. Taking these steps towards a larger community is, however, a necessary risk. Without this risk, we will submit – not to the power of God – but to the "new barbarians," the forces of intolerance and terror. But with the courage to reach out to the other comes a new hope, and toward this hope we strive.

Why can't we see that what we share is far greater than what divides us? Surely the truth of the Spirit is much bigger than any of us can imagine! Surely the issues that threaten our peoples – warfare, environmental devastation, social injustice, poverty, malnutrition, disease, lack of access to education – can only be addressed if we join together and freely contribute the wisdom and creativity our unique religious traditions have to offer! Without question, peace is the great imperative of our day, and the religions hold the key to it. Swiss Catholic theologian Hans Kung is surely correct in his conviction that there can be "no peace among the nations without peace among the religions; no peace among the religions without dialogue among the religions."[9] And surely our religions themselves have nothing to fear from this dialogue, but stand only to grow, to be enriched, deepened, and transformed.

## The World's Potluck:
## Bringing a Christian Dish to the World's Table

So what does a Christian have to bring to the table of dialogue? What can we offer our interfaith neighbors that may be received by them as a gift and as a contribution to the greater goal of peace and cooperation? That, of course, is no simple question. I belong to a faith tradition that all too often has abandoned the simple example and teaching of Jesus and that has linked itself to worldly, imperial powers, oppressive political structures, and absolutist, triumphal evangelism. Christianity can offer little that will not be viewed with suspicion by many in the larger family of faiths. Some may even rebuff any offer from Christians with a "thanks, but no thanks." Given Christianity's checkered history, this should not be surprising. But for Christians to give up and to retreat into a self-imposed exile from the world would not only be cowardly, but uncompassionate if Christians truly believe in the treasure that they have received. To be indeed a priceless treasure, it need not be the only treasure. It need not be the only truth to be an empowering, ennobling truth which is meant to be shared with all the world in a spirit of humility, generosity, and respect.

So what is this treasure, this truth? I was once asked this question in the context of an interfaith dialogue with some close Muslim friends. They asked me this question: *"What in your faith tradition and in your own practice of faith would you most wish those from other traditions to know?"* I had never really thought about that before. I knew what mattered to me personally, but having a modern, private conception of faith, I had never really considered sharing my view with someone who wasn't already a Christian. And I certainly was loathe to offend my friends or to say anything that would make them uncomfortable. But they asked the question, and I had to answer them.

My answer, I said, has to do with the Cross. Yes, the Cross – offense, stumbling block, ubiquitous symbol ... at the front of a Christian sanctuary, emblazoned on Crusaders' shields, raised over the dead in our cemeteries ... the Cross. Proceeding almost apologetically, I explained that the Cross I knew was not a sign of religious absolutism or of hatred. Many in the past had done evil in its shadow, I said, but in committing such acts – however sincerely or zealously – they only showed that they knew nothing of what it meant. Continuing, I said that to me the symbol of the Cross was an ever-present reminder of a God who is not remote from suffering and from the pain and alienation that we all feel. In fact, the symbol of the cross reaches beyond Christianity. It speaks of a God who is larger than the Church, greater than Christianity as a religion; it bespeaks a God who created the universe and everyone in it. This vision of the God beyond the cross invites all people to share in his infinite love for creation.

Further, the cross emboldens me to imagine a God who is *on our side* – not on the side of this or that agenda or program or government or army – but on the side of all who suffer ... not sitting on the sidelines or watching from above in the lofty box seats of Heaven, but engaged and involved, and empowering all who would take up that Cross as their own to stand in solidarity with the hurting, the alienated, the victims of any power that opposes the rule of Love, regardless of who those victims are. Regardless of what name they give to the Sacred, regardless of what they look like, regardless of whom they love. That was what it meant and means to me, I said, and that was what I would offer – as a Christian – to my Muslim friends.

My gift, my offering, was received with gladness.

# Notes

1.  Dietrich Bonhoeffer, *Letters and Papers from Prison*, edited by Eberhard Bethge. Enlarged edition (New York: Collier Books, 1971), pp. 369-370.
2.  From William Wordsworth's poem "The Tables Turned." Found online at http://www.bartleby.com/145/ww134.html
3.  I Corinthians 1:18-25, NIV
4.  I Corinthians 11: 23-26, NIV
5.  *The Presbyterian Hymnal* (Louisville, KY: Westminster/John Knox Press, 1990), Hymn # 264, "When in Our Music God is Glorified," verses 1 and 2.
6.  Found online: http://www.journeywithjesus.net/PoemsAndPrayers/Teresa_Of_Avila_Christ_Has_No_/Body.shtml>
7.  Ken Wilber, *A Theory of Everything: An Integral Vision for Business, Politics, Science and Spirituality* (Boston: Shambhala, 2000), p. 1. Such ideas have captured the universal religious imagination; see, for example, the excellent essay by Turkish Muslim scholar M. Fethullah Gulen, "At the Threshold of a New Millennium," in M. Fethullah Gulen: Essays, Perspectives, Opinions (Rutherford, NJ: The Light, 2002), pp. 21-31.
8.  Albert Camus, "The Unbeliever and Christians" in *Resistance, Rebellion, and Death*, translated by Justin O'Brien (New York: Alfred A. Knopf, 1961), p. 71.
9.  Hans Kung, *Global Responsibility: In Search of a New World Ethic* (New York: Crossroad, 1991), p. 138. See also the resources available on the web site of the Global Ethic Foundation.

# Glossary

**Baptism** – A rite of initiation into the Christian faith. The practice of baptism in the Catholic Church and in Reformed churches is offered to infants, children and adults; the administration of the water is either by sprinkling, pouring or immersion.

**Bible** – the sacred scriptures containing both the Old and New Testaments

**Christianity** -- this word refers to the churches and individuals who believe that Jesus Christ is the revelation of God to humanity and that through him the world has been reconciled to God. Within this inclusive term there are many different forms of Christianity.

**Catholic** – refers to the Roman Catholic Church. It is an institution with priests as leaders of congregations, bishops as overseers and the Pope in Rome who is the head of the church. The Apostle Peter was considered to be the first Pope.

**Eastern Orthodox** – a branch of the church which split off from the Roman Church in 1054. The Orthodox Church considers other churches to be schismatic and, in some cases, holding false doctrines.

**Disciple** – generally, a learner; anyone seeking to learn and follow the way of Christ.

**Eternal life** – the promise of Jesus to all who follow him. The hope of eternal life is the antidote to the fear of death. The author of the Gospel of John penned, "For God so loved the world that he gave his only Son that whoever believes in him should not perish but have eternal life." (John 3:16)

**Lord's Supper** – also know as Communion or the Eucharist. Refers to the last meal that Jesus had with his disciples when he instituted the practice of breaking bread and drinking wine together. He said of the bread, "this is my body," of the wine, "this is my blood." This practice was the Christian equivalent of the Jewish celebration of Passover, commemorating the Angel of the Lord "passing over" the Jewish male children in Egypt before the Exodus.

**Multiculturalism** – this term is neither religious nor spiritual but refers to a situation in which all religions find themselves in the twenty-first century. Through global travel, the Internet and migration, people of various cultures are meeting each other. In this century there is a growing need for understanding and cooperation in a multicultural world. In the United States, for example, the peoples to whom Christian churches once sent missionaries are no longer across the sea; they are next door.

**Protestant Christianity** – the movement which began in the sixteenth century in Europe in protest of many doctrines and practices of the Roman Catholic Church. The leaders of this movement – Martin Luther, John Calvin, Ulrich

Zwingli and others – were called the Reformers as they sought reform of the Church according to their view of the teachings of the Bible. Protestants believe that the Bible, not the Pope, provides the supreme authority for Christians. Critics of these Protestants suggest that the Bible has for them become a paper pope. This position on authority has led to different views of the sacraments, salvation and authority within the church.

> **Conservative** – the conservative Christian generally resists change; the interpretation of the Bible tends to be literal and traditional. The conservative often sees change as compromising the integrity of the faith. With respect to social issues the conservative will maintain traditional beliefs.

> **Liberal** – denotes a position on the Bible which is more generous in its interpretation, making room for change. Issues like divorce, sexual orientation and women's rights have all produced both conservative and liberal views.

**Reformed Tradition** – A distinctive stream of Protestant Christianity with roots in the teachings of the French reformer John Calvin (1509-1564), emphasizing the sovereignty of God over all things and the centrality of the teaching and preaching of the Word of God in scripture.

**Resurrection** – the Christian doctrine that Jesus of Nazareth, after his execution, rose from the dead by the power of God.

**Sacraments** – practices that commemorate important events. Generally, a sacrament is a natural practice that is given a spiritual meaning; for example, water for drinking becomes the water of initiation into the faith through baptism. Protestants limit the Sacraments to two (Baptism and the Lord's Supper). The Roman Catholic Church recognizes those, plus Reconciliation, Confirmation, Marriage, Holy Orders and Anointing of the Sick, for a total of seven.

**Sanctuary** – The principal worship space in a Christian church, usually regarded as especially sacred.

**Sermon** – a part of Christian worship in which the minister preaches on a biblical text (from the Old and/or New Testaments) and interprets in a manner that addresses the minds and hearts of each worshipper.

**Trinity** – The Christian doctrine, variously interpreted, that God consists of three persons (e.g., the Father, the Son, and the Holy Spirit), who are yet perfectly one God.

# For Further Reading

Armstrong, Karen. *A History of God*. New York: Alfred A. Knopf, 1993.

Borg, Marcus J. *The Heart of Christianity: Rediscovering a Life of Faith*. HarperSanFrancisco, 2003.

Foster, Richard J. Prayer: *Finding The Heart's True Home*. HarperSanFrancisco, 1992.

Johnson, Ben C. and Baker, Brant D. *The Jesus Story*. Geneva Press, 2000.

Johnson, Ben Campbell. *The God Who Speaks: Learning the Language of God*. Grand Rapids, MI:Eerdmans, 2000.

Lamott, Anne. *Traveling Mercies: Some Thoughts on Faith*. New York: Anchor Books, 2000.

Lewis, C. S. *Mere Christianity*. New York: Macmillan, 1993.

*Islamic Sacred Space*

# CHAPTER THREE

# The Mosque: Sacred Space of Muslims

---

## Imam Plemon T. El-Amin

*"The Mosques of Allah shall be visited and maintained by such as believe in God and the Last Day, establish regular prayers, practice regular charity and fear none except Allah. It is they who are expected to be on true guidance."*
                                                                    -Qur'an 9:18

**The most pleasurable and inspiring place for Muslims is the Masjid** (Mosque). Muslims go there to pray, reflect, praise and plead, to seek knowledge, guidance, inspiration and forgiveness, alone and in congregation. The Masjid is the center for worship, and since Islam regards both the practice and purpose of life to be worship, (Q 51:56), the Masjid becomes the center for spiritual, intellectual, cultural, social, and political affairs. The Islamic tradition is to establish a Mosque first, anticipating that the neighborhood, village, town and city will soon emerge and radiate around it.

Muslims are obligated to pray five times every day. These five obligatory prayers at prescribed times generate a daily ebb and flow of men and women pulsating in and out of the Masjid. It is the meeting place, the destination, the home-away-from-home, the retreat, the sanctuary, the center of society, and first and foremost, the House of Allah (God).

As one approaches a Masjid, usually the first thing one sees is a high tower called a minaret. Muslims are summoned to the five prayers with a verbal chanting by the prayer caller, the *Muezzin*. Before electronic amplification, the

*Muezzin* climbed up into the minaret enabling his voice to be heard in the distance. Nowadays, the call is made from inside, and loud speakers are situated in the minarets. The call reverberates throughout the neighborhood, exclaiming prayer time has arrived and explaining the purpose and motivation:

*"Allahu Akbar, Allahu Akbar"*
*G-d is Greater, G-d is Greater*

*"Allahu Akbar, Allahu Akbar"*
*G-d is Greater, G-d is Greater*

*"Ash-hadu an laa ilaha ill-Allah"*
*I bear witness that nothing deserves to be worshipped except G-d*

*"Ash-hadu an laa ilaha ill-Allah"*
*I bear witness that nothing deserves to be worshipped except G-d*

*"Ash-hadu anna Muhammadan Rasulu-llah"*
*I bear witness that Muhammad is the Messenger of G-d*

*"Ash-hadu anna Muhammadan Rasulu-llah"*
*I bear witness that Muhammad is the Messenger of G-d*

*"Hayya ala-s-salah, Hayya ala-s-salah"*
*Come to prayer, Come to prayer*

*"Hayya ala-l-falah, Hayya ala-l-falah"*
*Come to cultivation, Come to cultivation*

*"Allahu Akbar, Allahu Akbar"*
*G-d is Greater, G-d is Greater*

*"Laa ilaha ill-Allah"*
*There is no god but G-d*

Five times every day, a voice from among the people chants these exact phrases in Arabic, breaking the silence of dawn, the heat of noon, the activity

**74**

of the afternoon, the beauty of the sunset, and the darkness of night – voices as diverse as the population, sometimes startling, sometimes mesmerizing, at times overwhelming, and always inspiring bodies, minds, and souls to respond to God.

## Entering the Masjid

The words Masjid and Mosque are interchangeable because they are the same word in different languages. Mosque is the French derivation of the Arabic word Masjid, but the root meaning of the word is only preserved in the Arabic. Masjid is a place for Sajdah or prostrating, a place for bowing down. So when one enters a Masjid, the predominate characteristics are open space and serenity, few chairs if any, no pews or benches, scarce furnishings, and instead waves of carpet beckoning one to bow and prostrate.

Before praying, however, Muslims perform the ritual ablution called "*wudu,*" where the hands, mouth, nostrils, face, ears, head, arms and feet are washed with pure water to prepare one's consciousness and spirit for prayer. At some Masajid (pl.), fountains surrounded by stools are located in the courtyard for this purpose, while at others special areas are designed inside for this aspect of ritual purification.

As worshipers enter the actual prayer area, specifically called the *Musallan* (the place of prayer), they remove their shoes, and step in on their right foot. Tradition connects the removal of shoes to the Biblical and Qur'anic command from G-d to Moses (Exodus 3:5, Qur'an 20:12) to take off his shoes for he was entering sacred or holy ground. Coming in upon the right foot reminds one to be conscious of G-d and the environment of worship.

The openness, tranquility, and simplicity embrace those who come to pray. Few furnishings are visible, perhaps a podium or more likely a wooden mimbar composed of three or more steps that the Imam mounts to deliver a Friday Khutbah (teaching). There is calligraphy adorning the walls, words and verses from the Qur'an written in the most beautiful script imaginable, flowing from right to left and around, glorifying and praising G-d, the Most High, and reminding men and women that their obligation of worship is really a gift and a favor that unfolds for them the wonders and great benefits of life.

## Orientation

Every Masjid is oriented towards Mecca and the ancient place of worship built by Prophet Abraham and his son Ismail, called the Kaaba. Allah, the Most High, reveals in the Qur'an:

> "The first House (of worship) appointed for mankind was that at Bakkah (Mecca), full of blessings and of guidance for all beings. In it are manifest signs, such as the Station of Abraham, whoever enters it attains security. Pilgrimage thereto is a duty people who can afford the journey owe to Allah. But if any deny faith, Allah stands not in need of any of His creatures."

-Qur'an 3:96-97

These verses establish the importance of Mecca, and instruct believers to perform the Hajj (pilgrimage) to the Kaaba built by Abraham. Every year, at the appointed lunar calendar dates, millions of Muslim women and men travel to Arabia to fulfill the last pillar of Islam, to complete the Hajj (pilgrimage) to Mecca at least once in their lifetime. (Qur'an 2:196-203). People leave the comforts of their homes and surroundings, and traverse by land, air, and sea to enter into an ocean of humanity for 2 -3 weeks with sparse provisions in the desert heat of Arabia, to fulfill the obligation of connecting to the earliest of sacrifices and pronouncements of faith fulfilled by Prophet Abraham, his son Ismail, and his wife Hagar.

The ancient stone house that is the center of the Pilgrimage, the Kaaba, is described as the first house of worship built to accommodate the whole human congregation. This simple cubic structure, perhaps 60 feet by 60 feet by 60 feet, is not designed to hold people inside of it; rather, the worship occurs outside and around it. The Kaaba becomes the epicenter and orientation for multiple radiating circles of human beings performing prayers with it as the hub. Over the years, the Masjid surrounding the Kaaba has been architecturally expanded and elaborated upon to such an extent that its beauty and expanse has no comparison in the world. It can hold almost one million people at a time, and the predominating white, black, and rose marble is exquisite, softened by the artistry of Arabian rugs and the openness of majestic desert skies. This is the Masjid that orients all Masajid.

When one enters any Mosque, there is a clear orientation marked by an encasement or portal on a specific wall called the Mihrab. The Mihrab identifies the direction of the Kaaba or the Qibla (orientation for prayer). The direction in the U.S. is east and northeast, in South Africa it is northerly, in China it is southerly, and in India westerly. When Muslims pray, they form various arcs

**76**

of gigantic circles, similar to the human circles in Mecca, in such a way that if any prayer line was fully protracted, it would join arcs from country to country, forming huge circles, always with Mecca as the center.

It is important to note that every prayer ends asking G-d to exalt Muhammad and his followers as He exalted Abraham and his followers, and to bless Muhammad and his followers as He blessed Abraham and his followers. This connection and orientation towards the life, service, example, intellect, and sacrifice of Prophet Abraham in the Muslim life and worship is too often overlooked or minimized by others.

The Hajj is not complete until the pilgrims, still dressed in the simplest two wraps of white cloth, return in mass from the desert of Arafat to the Sacred Precincts of Masjid Al-Haraam. Retracing the steps, trials, sacrifices and victory of Prophet Abraham, they enter the Mosque as a multitude of humanity, and they circumambulate the Ancient House he built with his son Ismail seven times, testifying:

*"Labbaika Allah-umma labbaika, La sharika la-ka labbaika"*
**"Here I am O Allah! Here I am! No partner have You! Here I am!"**

And Allah reveals in the Qur'an:

*"And remember that Abraham was tried by his Lord with certain Commands which he fulfilled. G-d said: 'I will make you an Imam to the Nations.' Abraham pleaded: 'And also (Imams) from among my offspring!' Allah answered: 'But My Promise is not within reach of the corrupt.'*

*"Remember We made the House a place of assembly for men and a place of safety. So take you the Station of Abraham as a place of prayer. And We covenanted with Abraham and Ismail that they should sanctify My House for those who compass it round, or use it as a retreat, or bow, or prostrate themselves (therein in prayer)."*
-Qur'an 2:124-125

To be in Masjid Al-Haraam during Hajj transports and immerses one into what registers as an alternative reality. The beauty of the Masjid and the simplicity of the Kaaba touch the soul, but it is the ocean of people that transforms the reality: witnessing, from within, humanity fluidly whirling step by step around the Kaaba, and only pausing in place when the call to stand for each of the five daily prayers is pronounced. The whirlpool of humanity becomes still. The cascading circles emanate, and the flow transforms into choreographed bowing, prostrating, and standing, replicating the opening, closing and opening again of a beautiful rose or exotic flower. With the traditional obligatory greeting of G-d's Peace to those on the right and then to those on the left that concludes each prayer, immediately the flower liquidates into the swirling flow of human beings praising the One Lord of the House, of the Humanity, and of the known and unknown Universe.

## The Prayer

The actual prayer service that occurs in the Masjid is called *Salah*, and can be performed in any clean place or environment. The Salah is prescribed in many Qur'anic verses, and its specificity is established in the practices of Prophet Muhammad (G-d's peace and blessings be upon him). After the *Adhan* (call to prayer), a shortened version is uttered called the *Iqama*, which instructs Muslims to stand and form the ranks or lines for Salah. The Salah involves every aspect of the worshipper: the body, the mind, the soul, the spirit, and one's neighbor. The lines and ranks are formed tightly, behind the Imam, foot to foot, shoulder to shoulder with those next to you on each side, standing erect, and focusing down to the spot where you will soon prostrate your head. This close arrangement is the governing factor behind the separation of males and females for the Salah. The preservation of modesty and the minimizing of distractions enjoin that men and women perform these prayers in separated groupings.

It begins with hands raised to both ears, a sign that one is ready to listen, and with the proclamation "Allahu Akbar," G-d is Greater. The language of the Salah is Qur'anic Arabic. Certainly, Muslims understand that G-d hears every language and every soul and heart whether verbal or silent, but the uniformity of praying to and seeking guidance, forgiveness and mercy from the One G-d in one language among intricately diverse souls accents and uplifts the universal commonality of humanity. As different and distinct that people may perceive themselves to be, before G-d those differences vanish.

Every Salah begins with the same seven verses from Qur'an, the Opening Chapter called *Al-Fatiha*:

*"With Allah's Name, Merciful Benefactor, Merciful Redeemer*

*Praise be to Allah, the Cherisher and Sustainer of the Worlds,*
*Merciful Benefactor, Merciful Redeemer*
*Master of the Day of Judgment*
*You alone do we worship and Your Aid we seek.*
*Show us the Straight Way,*
*The Way of those on whom you have bestowed Your Grace, those*
*whose (portion) is not wrath,*
*And who go not astray."*
*Amin*

After this recitation from the Imam (prayer leader), he can recite any verse or portion from the Qur'an because every verse, or word for that matter, is considered a sacred revelatory prayer.

That recitation will be followed by the call "Allahu Akbar" (G-d is Greater), which alerts the congregation to move to the next position and reminds everyone that whatever your perception of G-d, Allah is greater than your image or estimation. At this point, everyone bows their backs with hands on knees, and recites three times in Arabic, "Glory to My Lord the Most Great." With the sound of the Imam's voice proclaiming "G-d answers those who praise Him," the congregation stands erect, saying "O Allah, for You is the Praise." And with the Imam's proclamation of "Allahu Akbar," everyone descends their foreheads, knees and hands to the floor, assuming the position of ultimate humility called *Sajdah* (prostration). Remember, this is the position after which the Masjid is named; it is this moment that captures the purpose of the Mosque, the "Place of Submissive Prostration" or the "Place of Bowing Down."

In this position of humility, the worshipper proclaims three (3) times, "Glory to my Lord, the Most High," then is reminded "Allahu Akbar" – G-d is greater than even what you are perceiving in this humble position. The worshipper then sits erect, praises G-d, pronouncing "Allahu Akbar" and returns to the position of Sajdah, giving glory to the Most High before declaring again that G-d is Greater, and rising to one's feet erect to begin the service movements once again if it's the Morning Prayer; three (3) additional times if it's the noon, afternoon, or night prayers; and two (2) additional times if it is the sunset prayer.

This service, five times daily, is central to the life of the Muslim. It can be performed at home, at work, or in any clean environment. Prophet Muhammad said the whole earth is a Masjid, making Muslims very comfortable offering prayers in parks and by the side of the road. Still, the preferred place for this daily sacred service is, without a doubt, the Masjid, making it the central station of exchange for the ebb and flow of drops, streams, and oceans of diverse yet connected humanity throughout the world. This prominent and central place of the Masjid in the daily life of 1.5 billion Muslims has inspired amazing structures and architectural wonders, as well as practical utilitarian Mosques that seamlessly blend into the other buildings of the neighborhood.

## The Prophet's Mosque

The Prophet Muhammad (May G-d's peace and blessings be upon him) said, "Whoever builds a Mosque, desiring only Allah's Pleasure, Allah builds for him the likeness of it in Paradise." (Bukhari 8:65). And Allah reveals in Qur'an (9:08) that *"a Mosque whose foundation was laid from the first day on piety, it is more worthy of one's standing forth (for prayer) within. In it are men who love to be purified and Allah loves those who make themselves pure."*

## Medina

The Prophet's Mosque that he helped to build with his own hands in Medina, Arabia, remains one of the most beautiful in the world. During Prophet Muhammad's time, this Mosque was a simple structure made of sun-baked bricks, with a partial roof of palm leaves supported by columns of palm tree trunks. It was surrounded by a vast courtyard that accommodated individual and family tents. Today this marvelous structure of white, gray, and black marble, accented throughout with green and blue tiles, occupies the entire past boundaries of the original oasis town. Its retractable roof facilitates the comfort of the 500,000 worshippers the Masjid can hold at any given time. On every Muslim's list of Mosques to visit, without doubt, the Mosque surrounding the Kaaba in Mecca (Masjid Al-Haram) is first, and the Prophet's Masjid (Masjid An-Nabawi) is second.

## Jerusalem

The third important Mosque to Muslims is named in Qur'an as Masjid Al-Aqsa, the farthest Mosque, in Jerusalem.
*"Glory to (Allah) Who did take His servant for a Journey by night from the Sacred Mosque (Mecca) to the Farthest Mosque*

*(Jerusalem), whose precincts We did bless, in order that We might show him some of Our Signs, for He is the One Who Hears and Sees."*
                                                                    -Qur'an 17:1

This verse references the spiritual night journey of Prophet Muhammad from Mecca to Jerusalem around 622 A.D. The site that is called the Farthest Mosque was the razed site of Solomon's Temple, and at that time was regarded as the *Qibla* (direction) for Muslims' clandestine (out of fear of persecution) prayers.   Prophet Muhammad recognized a strong connection between his calling and the missions of Jesus, Moses, David and Solomon and regarded Jerusalem as the common spiritual center.   Shortly after this night journey, the Prophet migrated from Mecca (*Hijra*) upon an invitation of the people of Medina, and soon received the Qur'anic revelation to turn towards Mecca as the Qibla for prayer orientation.   This instruction simultaneously distinguished the Muslim community from previous religious movements and clearly connected them with the Prophet Abraham.

This change also would enable Jerusalem to be preserved and protected as a city for Jews, Christian, and Muslims instead of the spiritual center for 1.5 billion Muslims today.

Still, the visual centerpiece of Jerusalem is the Dome of the Rock on the plateau of the Haram al-Sharif (the Noble Sanctuary) in the Old City. It is believed that the Prophet Muhammad ascended into the Heavens from the rock that this beautiful structure covers.  Most Muslims regard it as a Masjid, even though some see it as a shrine, yet all who visit it offer prayers inside. It is an octagonal masterpiece, crowned with a gold-plated aluminum dome, and adorned with bluish stucco and tile mosaics, along with marble and stained glass panels. Its beauty is captivating.  Built in 691 AD, it remains the pride of Jerusalem.

Upon the same plateau of the Haram al-Sharif (the Noble Sanctuary) is Al-Aqsa Mosque (the Farthest Mosque).  Built in 715 AD, its very plain outside appearance disguises an inner-sanctuary of vivid colors and light intermingling and reverberating off and upon marble columns, wooden rafters, paneled ceilings, mosaic walls, and lush carpets.  The Friday prayers attract between 50,000 and 100,000 worshippers, and many of them remain to perform the travelers' prayers, disclosing that they are not residents of Jerusalem.  Muslims regard the Haram al-Sharif as sacred grounds not just because of the Al-Aqsa Mosque or the Dome of the Rock, but also because it is the place of the Temple built by Solomon, which in Qur'an is called "the Farthest Place of Prostration."

## Masajid

After these top three Mosques or Masajid, the list of favorites begins to differ according to whom you ask. My favorites that I have personally visited and offered prayers in are:

• The Blue Mosque (Sultanahmet Mosque) in Istanbul, Turkey. This seventeenth-century masterpiece dominates the skyline with its six minarets and a cascade of domes spilling down from a great central dome. The 20,000 blue tiles that decorate the interior in abstract patterns are responsible for the name, while the 260 stained glass windows bring in light that is both subtle and exuberant at once.

• The Suleymaniye Mosque, also in Istanbul, is the sixteenth-century work of the extraordinary Ottoman architect Mimar Sinan on behalf of Sultan Suleyman the Magnificent. It is the largest in Istanbul and overlooks the city and the Golden Horn from one of the highest locations.

• The Hassan II Mosque in Casablanca, Morocco, which was built in 1993 on land reclaimed from the Atlantic Ocean. Fifty percent of the floor space extends over the ocean, which can be seen through glass flooring. For prayers the Masjid can accommodate 25,000 inside and 80,000 people in the courtyard . Its single minaret is 689 ft tall.

• Al-Hambra in Granada , Spain, and the Great Mosque of Cordoba, Spain, are favorites even though neither is utilized as a Masjid today. Still, the beauty and splendor of each is well-preserved and inspiring.

• Baitul Mukarram in Dhaka, Bangladesh, is a National Mosque built in 1960 and one of the largest and most beautiful Masajid in Bangladesh.

• Masjid Negara in Kuala Lumpur, Malaysia, is a National Mosque that is  beautiful and amazing, as is the Sultan Salahuddin Abdel Aziz Mosque in Shah Alam, Malaysia.

Mosques that are on my "must see soon" list are:

The Great Mosque of Djenné in Mali

The Abuja National Mosque in Nigeria

The Great Mosque of Kano in Nigeria

The Faisal Mosque in Islamabad, Pakistan, and

The Great Mosque at Touba in Senegal

Of course my two favorites are right here in Atlanta:  Masjid Al-Farooq and the Atlanta Masjid of Al-Islam.  Masjid Al-Farooq captures the classical Islamic architecture of Cordoba and Morocco while embracing modernity. The spiraling minaret and the dual copper domes can be seen from various vantage points in the city. The inner courtyard overlooks downtown in one direction with Cordoba-inspired arches beckoning one to enter the Masjid on the opposite side. The inner sanctuary exudes peace, beauty, and adoration of Allah, the Most High.

While the Atlanta Masjid of Al-Islam is no comparison architecturally, it exemplifies openness, transparency, functionality, practicality, and most importantly, community. The renovated property is clearly the center focus of the area, with shops, businesses, schools, homes, and activities radiating out and around it. It is well integrated into the neighborhood and sustains community intermingling, interaction, and vibrancy seven days each week from dawn until the dark of night. The call to prayer enlivens and regulates the entire community, both Muslim and non-Muslim alike.

Regardless of the location or the level of grandeur, every Mosque is a place where Muslims of any ethnicity, age, gender, and political persuasion are welcome to enter and worship the Lord of all the worlds, Who is Unseen, Uncontained, Omnipotent, Merciful, and Forgiving.

*"And who is more unjust than he who forbids access to the Mosques of Allah, that His Name should be celebrated?"*

-Qur'an 2:114

The Masjid is the training ground for equality and brotherhood. Five times daily, men and women of diverse backgrounds, occupations, and interests come to the Masjid where there are no pre-assigned seats or positions of distinction. Everyone enters as a servant of G-d and as a brother or sister of the believers that happen to surround them for that particular prayer. Color does not matter, class has no bearing, dress and style are ignored, generation gaps are closed and the human essence stands shoulder to shoulder, foot to foot, bowing, prostrating, reciting, praising, greeting, hugging, and returning into the world of occupation infused with a rejuvenating dosage of G-d consciousness and human fraternity. It is reported that Prophet Muhammad said:

*"Tell me if there is a stream at the door of one of you, in which he bathes five times every day, what do you say, will it leave anything of his dust? They said: It would not leave anything of his dirt. He said: This is the likeness of the five prayers, with which Allah blots out (all) faults."*

-Sahih Bukhari

The Masjid is first and foremost a place for purification and prayer. In Al-Islam, the prime cause and effect of purification is the clear belief and commitment to the Oneness and Universality of G-d. It is not a narrow belief or conceptualization, but neither is it confused or vague. Allah is the Creator, Preserver, Sustainer and Judge of everything that exists. Islam asserts that there are only two existences: G-d and Creation and that only G-d is External, Absolute, and Independent while Creation is temporal, dependent, and vanishing. The Qur'an states that Allah, the Most High, is actually "the Only Reality" or "the Only Truth." Most Muslims are quick to emphasize that this is not a Muslim G-d, but the G-d of Adam, Noah, Abraham, Moses, Jesus, and Muhammad (peace be upon all of them and all of the Prophets and Messengers of Allah).

I am reminded of the words of Archbishop Desmond Tutu that seemed to startle the mostly Christian audience gathered at the New Ebenezer Baptist Church in Atlanta. In the middle of a wonderful description of the faith and sacrifice of South Africans to move almost immediately from apartheid to reconciliation, he felt the need to tell his audience of faithful people appreciating what faith and religion can do: "You know," he quietly murmured in his Anglican-African accent, "G-d is not a Christian." A great silence of profound contemplation resonated upon the people's hearts and minds as if they had heard those words for the very first time. No, G-d is not a Christian, a Muslim, a Jew, nor a Hindu or Buddhist, a Male nor Female, but G-d is Real and always Present, and answers the prayers of the sincere and fulfills the aspirations of the good and decent.

The greatest sin in Al-Islam is to knowingly distort, confuse, complicate, disguise, or reject this distinctive universally monotheistic view of G-d. With that in mind, the Qur'an declares:

> "It is not for such as join gods with Allah, to visit or maintain the Mosques of Allah while they witness against their own souls to infidelity. The works of such bear no fruit, in the Fire shall they dwell. The Mosques of Allah shall be visited and maintained by such as believe in Allah and the Last Day, establish regular prayers and practice regular charity, and fear none except G-d. It is they who are expected to be on true guidance."
>
> -Qur'an 9:17-18

Although some take these verses to restrict the Mosques to Muslims only, the

Qur'an applies the term Muslim (one who submits) much more generously, identifying Noah (10:72), Abraham (22:78), Moses (10:90), Joseph (12:101) , Jesus (3:52) and their close companions as Muslims who submit and surrender to the Will of G-d. Therein, for many, the Masjid is sanctuary for any who believe in G-d and the Last Day and do good. The late and profound Muslim American Imam and Leader, Warith Deen Mohammed, captured this spirit in these words:

> "The time to see each other as enemies is out. We must be pleased as Muslims to see good Christians being good Christians, good Jews being good Jews, as well as good Buddhists, good Hindus, and others. We want success for any who believe in goodness and who invest in the human life and being. We must come together and trust, respect, and appreciate our common essence and sensitivities as Human Beings."

He often referenced the following Qur'anic verse to give support and understanding to his position:

> "And hold fast all together by the rope which G-d (stretches out for you) and be not divided among yourselves. And remember with gratitude G-d's Favor on you, for you were enemies and He joined your hearts in love, so that by His Grace you became brethren. And you were on the brink of the Pit of Fire and He saved you from it. Thus does G-d make His Signs clear to you that you may be guided."
>
> -Qur'an 3:10

Imam W. Deen Mohammed said he believed the word Muslim was revealed to replace the word human, to reconnect people once again to the sacred worth and dignity of one another.

Throughout Qur'an human nature and destiny are described as Muslim, but as mentioned earlier, a sincere perusal of the Qur'anic use of the word leads one to conclude that many who are not considered by themselves or others to be a part of the Islamic faith do in fact fall within the definition of Muslim as one who submits to G-d and seeks peace. Not only does the Qur'an encourage freedom of religion – "Let there be no compulsion in religion. Truth stands out clear from error." (Q. 2:256). But the scripture revealed to Prophet Muhammad over a 23-year period (610-633 AD) recognizes and supports the religions of others.

"Those who believe (in the Qur'an) and those who follow the Jewish (scriptures) and the Christians and the Sabians – and any who believe in Allah and the Last Day and work righteousness shall have their reward with their Lord. On them shall be no fear nor shall they grieve."

-Qur'an 2:62

G-d, the Most High, even instructs Muslims to fight the aggressor who threatens other houses of worship.

*"To those against whom war is made, permission is given (to fight) because they are wronged. And verily, Allah is Most Powerful for their aid. (They are) those who have been expelled from their homes in defiance of right (for no cause) except that they say: 'Our Lord is G-d.' If G-d did not check one set of people by means of another, there would surely have been destroyed Monasteries, Churches, Synagogues and Mosques in which the Name of G-d is commemorated in abundant measure. Allah will certainly aid those who aid His (Cause) – for verily Allah is Full of Strength, Exalted in Might."*

Qur'an 22:39-40

### The Friday Day of Assembly- Jumah

*"O you who believe! When the call is proclaimed to prayer on Friday (the Day of Assembly), hasten earnestly to the remembrance of Allah, and leave off business (and traffic). That is best for you if you but knew."*

-Qur'an 62:9

The primary worship day in Al-Islam is Friday immediately after the noon sun. Friday is the Day of Congregation called Jumah, meaning "to assemble" in Arabic. On this day every week, the beauty and charm of the Masjid is a distant second to the enormity and focus of the crowds of worshippers. Muslims regard Jumah as a duty they owe to G-d and a command to come together in fraternity and equality, and in mass. This prayer takes the place of the second daily prayer, which usually has four (4) Rakahs (movements). Jumah prayer only has two (2) Rakahs, but a sermon, called Khutbah (teaching) is offered in two (2) parts. Most Muslims regard these two speeches as substitutes for the two (2) movements that are absent on Friday, and therefore hold the words in the same esteem as prayer. It is tradition for the Imam to utilize the first part for the glorification and praise of Allah (the Most High), and to elevate and/or expand the worshippers' spiritual consciousness. The second part has customarily been used to address the community's needs, welfare, and social issues.

After the Khutbah, the Muezzin calls the people to stand and form the prayer ranks, and the Imam leads the congregation in the Jumah Salah, reciting from the Qur'an in Arabic. Although Muslims regard Friday as the most special day of any week, it is not considered a day of Sabbath. The Qur'an states:

*"And when the Prayer is finished, then may you disperse through the land and seek the bounty of Allah, and celebrate the praises of Allah often, that you may prosper."*

-Qur'an 62:10

In Al-Islam, the concept of G-d resting, tiring, slumbering, or sleeping is non-existent. Allah, the Most High, is always active, vigilant, and perpetually creating. Islam stresses that G-d is unlike and incomparable to anything in creation, and limitations inherent to human life are not applicable to G-d.

### Ramadan

The most special period of time at any and every Mosque is the Month of Ramadan.

*"Ramadan is the (month) in which was sent down the Qur'an as a guide to mankind and with clear (signs) for guidance and judgment (between right and wrong). So every one of you who is present (at his home) during the month should spend it in fasting...."*

-Qur'an 2:185

For 29 or 30 days every year of the lunar calendar, Muslims abstain from all food and drink from dawn to sunset. The lunar year, being 10-11 days shorter than the solar year, rotates through the solar calendar. This difference accommodates the movement of Ramadan through every season, allowing Muslims the benefits and difficulties of fasting under all conditions equally. In the summer, days are long, hot, and difficult, while in the winter, days are short, cold, and easy upon the one fasting.

In addition to the daylight fasting from food and drink, one abstains from intimate marital relationships. After sunset, food, drink, and marital intimacy are allowed with the caution of moderation. During the entire month, one must also strive to avoid lying, quarreling, backbiting, gossiping, cheating, anger, and abuses. Additional nighttime prayers are highly recommended, and large numbers of Muslims perform all of these prayers at the Masjid.

The Masjid overruns with Believers at the peak of their awareness and regard of G-d. During the nighttime prayer, called Tarawih, each night one-thirtieth of the Qur'an is recited, usually by a Hafis (one who memorized the whole of Qur'an). Therefore, by the end of the month of fasting, the whole community has heard, read, or recited all of Qur'an. Most Masajid provide meals at sunset, and the energy in the Mosque during Ramadan becomes deeply spiritual and gregarious at once.

Fasting is usually very personal, but when everyone is fasting, praying, and reading the exact same part of scripture every day for 30 days, it elevates into a community and global movement and worship. The food and drink serve as the catalyst to awaken the mind and the soul to the depth of life and being, individually and collectively.

The Masjid has a special glow during Ramadan. Every greeting, every kind word and gesture, every regardful thought and intent seems to carry the status of worship. Worldly pressures and concerns lose their weight, and the Word of G-d takes full precedence in all matters. The human spirit transcends the material demands, and life truly becomes worship. The physical demands of hunger, thirst, and even commerce become quiet, obedient requests that are easily accommodated in moderation.

The Prophet said, "Everything has its gateway and the gateway to worship is the prescribed fast." And Allah says in Qur'an 2:183:
"O you who believe, Fasting is prescribed to you as it was prescribed to those before you, that you may (learn) to be regardful of G-d."

After the successful 29-30 day fast of Ramadan, Muslims enjoy a three (3)-day celebration called Eid-al-Fitr (the Recurring Happiness of Nature). It begins with a mid-morning prayer in an open field or at the largest Masjid, and continues with daily feasts, celebrations, gift-giving, and entertainment. The other major celebration, called Eid-al-Adha (the Recurring Happiness of Sacrifice), comes after the completion of the Hajj (Pilgrimage) and is conducted with the same activities and spirit of celebration.

**The Place for Every Good**

The Masjid is the heart of Muslim life. The five (5) daily prayers bring the flow of human souls in and out of the Masjid chambers seeking guidance, direction, forgiveness, comfort, enlightenment, inspiration, answers, relief, ease, peace, wisdom, compassion, and mercy. They leave with lightened burdens and fresher perspectives to utilize and share among co-workers and associates, or perhaps only within their own souls, always conscious that, G-d willing, one will soon return to this place of revitalization or at least to the posture of sajdah (prostration and surrender).

Yet, the Masjid is much more than the waterhole in the midst of a material desert. The Muezzin calls "Hayya ala-s-salah" – "Come to prayer" – twice, and then "Hayya ala-l-falah" –"Come to Success/Cultivation" – twice, signifying that worship includes prayer and human development. The call is to the full and comprehensive human life. Allah, the Most High, says in Qur'an 28:77:

"And seek with all your means the Home of the Afterlife, but do not neglect your share of this World. And do you good, as Allah has been good to you, and seek not mischief in the land, for Allah loves not those who do mischief."

The Muslim is obligated to pursue through prayers and deeds the Paradise of Heaven and the good life of the World. In fact, the Qur'an connects the two and states that one who ignores the social needs around him is actually denying Judgment.

"See the one who denies the Judgment? Such is the one who repulses the Orphan, and encourages not the feeding of the indigent. So woe to the worshippers, who are neglectful of their prayers, those who (but want) to be seen (of men) but refuse (to supply even) neighborly needs."
-Qur'an 107

So the gathering of worshippers five (5) times a day involves more than prayer. The Mosque is the center for the exchange of ideas and education. Islamic schools begin in the Masjid and maintain connections even after they physically relocate. The Friday Sermon (Khutbah) should address the spiritual, intellectual and social needs and concerns of the community. It should set the stage for a week of dialogue, thought, exploration, and productivity.

The standing shoulder to shoulder and toe to toe breeds familiarity, interest and trust. Worshippers come to know one another and their occupations and involvements. Business and social relationships evolve. Partnerships and support systems are formed. Appointments and meetings are calibrated around prayer schedules at the Masjid.

During Prophet Muhammad's life, the Masjid in Medina served as the center for all political, educational, and cultural activities. There were always several circles of Believers in the Masjid being taught and discussing the Qur'an and the religion between prayers. Juridical affairs were presented and settled there. Even festivals and feasts were held on the grounds. Charity (Zakat) was collected and distributed from the Masjid.

Most Mosques today fully embrace this legacy established by the Prophet, that without ever taking away from the sacred character of the Masjid as primarily a place for prayer, the Mosque should serve as a center for every good and healthy human aspiration.

*"Say: My Lord has commanded Justice; and that you set your whole selves (to Him) at every time and place of prayer. And call upon Him, making your devotion sincere as in His Sight. Such as He created you in the beginning, so shall you return."*

-Qur'an 7:29

## Conclusion: The Oneness of G-d (Tauhid)

While there are only 2500 Mosques across America, there are more than 10 million Masajid throughout the world. These Mosques greatly differ in size, design, simplicity, extravagance, and age. They attract and accommodate every type of human being, with all of the cultural, ethnocentric, linguistic, historical, and social diversity imaginable. Yet, they are connected and intertwined by common beliefs, scripture, prayers, religious language, practices, and customs. They all regard Prophet Muhammad as the last in a line of Prophetic figures beginning with Adam, Noah, Abraham, Moses, Jesus, and numerous others. They orient each and every Mosque towards Mecca and the House of Worship first established by Prophet Abraham.

However, the ultimate and underlying belief and principle in Al-Islam and among Muslims is Tauhid, the Oneness of G-d. The short Qur'anic chapter Ikhlas (the Purity of Faith) that every Muslim recites frequently captures this extensive concept succinctly:

*"Say: He is Allah*
*The One and the Only,*
*Allah, the Eternal, Absolute*
*He gives not birth,*
*Nor is He borned,*
*And there is none like Him"*

-Qur'an Surah 112

Muslims are considered monotheists extraordinaire. G-d stands Alone, Independent, Self-Subsisting without needs (or even wants), always existing, the only true Entity, the only true Absolute, Undivided, Indivisible, a Single Unity from which everything that ever existed, everything that presently exists, and everything that ever will exist, receives its temporary existence through Allah's Mercy and Will and not G-d's Essence. Muslims believe that G-d has no associates, no partners, no family, and no sharers in Divinity. The Kalimah (statement of witness) that "baptizes" one into the religion states, "I bear witness that there is no god but G-d, and I bear witness that Muhammad is His Messenger." Muslims regard Muhammad and all other Prophets and Messengers as human beings called by G-d to share a revealed message with other human beings by word and deed. The oft-repeated proclamation of "Allahu Akbar" – G-d is Greater – captures the essence of Tauhid: no matter what you imagine, image, exegete, or estimate G-d to be, G-d is always Greater.

For these reasons, not only are there no images, statues, or paintings inside the Masjid, but also the activities and discussions should always be regardful of G-d's Divinity, Dignity, and Omnipresence.

*"And the Mosques (Masajid) are for G-d (Alone), so do not invoke*
*any other with Allah."*

-Qur'an 72:18

This clear and conscious belief in the Oneness and Absolute Independence of Allah brings Muslims to recognize their obligation to serve the G-d who is beyond need. Therefore the service must be directed towards the betterment of self, the family, the neighbor, the community, and the whole of creation. Worship, as well as the place of worship, is established to pursue, maintain and protect righteousness, decency, and justice for all.

This Islamic obligation of every Muslim and every Masjid is best captured in this oft-repeated verse from the Qur'an with which I conclude:

"It is not righteousness that you turn your face to the East or the West, but it is Righteousness to believe in Allah, and the Last Day, and the Angels, and the Book, and the Messengers; to spend of your substance out of the love of Him, for your kin, for orphans, for the needy, for the wayfarer, for those who ask, and for the ransom of slaves; to be steadfast in prayer and practice regular charity, to fulfill the contracts which you have made; and to be firm and patient in pain and adversity, and throughout all periods of panic. Such are the people of truth, the G-d fearing."

-Qur'an 2:177

# Glossary

**Allah** – Name of God in Arabic

**Adhan** – Melodic call to prayer, chanted aloud before each of the five daily prayers

**Hadith** – Sayings and practices of Prophet Muhammad (Peace and Blessings be upon him)

**Hafiz** – A person who has memorized the entire Qur'an

**Hajj** – The Pilgrimage to Mecca, an obligation upon every Muslim at least once in lifetime.

**Imam** – Person who leads the congregational prayers; the religious leader of a Muslim community

**Islam/Al-Islam** – Name of the religion which comes from the root word that means "Peace" and "Submission" to the Will of God

**Jumah** – The Friday Congregational Prayer

**Kaaba** – The cubical House of Worship constructed by Prophet Abraham and Ismail in the city of Mecca that is the focal point of every prayer.

**Khutbah** – The Friday sermon delivered at Jumah, or any lecture or speech.

**Masjid** – Place of worship for Muslims; same as Mosque

**Masajid** – Plural for Masjid in Arabic; same as Mosques

**Mecca** – City where Prophet Muhammad (Peace and Blessings be upon him) was born, and the religious center for Muslims

**Medina** – City where Prophet Muhammad (Peace and Blessings be upon him) immigrated from Mecca and established the first Muslim community

**Mihrab** – The niche inside the Masjid to show the direction of prayer.

**Minaret** – Tower where the call to prayer is performed

**Muezzin** – Person who performs the call to prayer

**Qur'an** – Holy Scripture revealed to Prophet Muhammad (Peace and Blessings be upon him) by God

**Ramadan** – Name of the ninth month in the Islamic calendar; designated for fasting

**Sajdah** – The position of prostration in each prayer.

**Salah** – The proper name for the Muslim prayer.

**Sunnah** – The tradition of Prophet Muhammad (Peace and Blessings be upon him)

**Tauhid** – The firm belief and declaration of the Oneness of God

**Wudu** – Ritual washing of the face, arms and feet by Muslims before prayer

# For Further Reading

Ahmed, Akbar. *Journey into Islam.* Washington, D.C.: Brookings Institution Press, 2007.

Armstrong, Karen. *Islam, A Short History.* New York: Random House Publishing, 2000).

_____ *Muhammad: A Biography of the Prophet.* New York: HarperCollins Publishers, 1993.

Aslan, Reza. *No God but God.* New York: Random House, 2005.

Esposito, John L. *Islam, The Straight Path.* New York: Oxford University Press, 1988.

Esposito, John L., and Mogahed, Dalia. *Who Speaks for Islam?* New York: Gallup Press, 2007.

Gulen, M. Fethullah. *Sufism, Key Concepts in the Practice of.* Fairfax, Virginia: The Fountain, 2000.

Thangaraj, M. Thomas. *Relating to People of Other Religions.* Nashville: Abingdon Press, 1997.

*The Meaning of The Holy Qur'an,* translation and commentary by Abdullah Yusuf Ali (1990 or earlier)

---

Be sure to read Appendix 2, "Meet Prophet Muhammad, Builder of the First Mosque" by Kemal Korucu and Mirkena Ozer, for additional information about the Prophet's early life.

*Hindu Sacred Space*

CHAPTER FOUR

# The Center/Temple: Sacred Space of Vedantists and Hindus

## Gillian Renault

*"Truth is one, sages call it by many names."* (Rig Veda 1.164.46)

**Welcome to the Sacred Space of Vedic religion!** It is my privilege to be your host as I introduce you to two expressions of the religion of India, commonly known as Hinduism. We will explore the sacred space of the Vedanta Center and the Hindu Temple. Both honor the ancient scriptures known as the Vedas. However, one is steeped in myth, culture and tradition; the other focuses on universal principles and philosophy, stripped of India's cultural overlays. Both welcome visitors of all faiths. Before we step inside either of these spaces, consider with me the faith itself.

In the West, we talk about organized religion. We are accustomed to religions based on the teachings of a charismatic individual such as Abraham, Mohammed, Buddha or Jesus. We are familiar with faiths that are led by a spiritual leader like the Pope, the Archbishop of Canterbury, or a group such as the Southern Baptist Convention. These leaders define church doctrine, are arbiters of morality, and shape the political structure of the faith. By comparison Hinduism is the most unorganized and decentralized religion in the world. It is not based on the life or teachings of an incarnation, messenger, or prophet. Instead, it is inspired by the Vedas, writings of several fully-realized sages that date back more than 5,000 years. It comprises six main philosophical systems and many loosely-structured teacher lineages which vary from one part of India to another.

## An Ancient Religion

How did Hinduism become so diverse and so decentralized?  Before the British arrived in India in the eighteenth century, the country was a conglomeration of many different nation-states with at least sixteen different languages and many dialects.  At that time, the religious ideas that permeated India were not even called Hinduism, but Sanatana Dharma (The Eternal Religion).  The British coined the phrase Hinduism to describe the faith they found there.

The term Hindu was first used by the Persian invaders in 4,000 BC who called the inhabitants around the Indus (or Sindhu) River Hindus instead of Sindhus.  To this day, the term Hindu, in its strictest sense, refers to persons born in India regardless of their faith.  Christians and Muslims living in India, however, prefer to call themselves Indians.  And Hindus believe that people of Hindu faith can be Indian or non-Indian.  The American-born children of Indian families who have emigrated to the United States will be American Hindus.  There is much debate in scholarly circles these days about the use of the words Hindu and Hinduism.  Is it a cultural or religious descriptor?  Is a practicing Christian born and living in India a Hindu?  Are Americans who practice yoga and meditation to be considered Hindus?  For the purposes of this discussion, we will use Hindu in its religious meaning in contrast with the cultural meaning, which includes other faiths in India.

Religion and culture are so intertwined in India it's impossible to know exactly where one stops and the other begins.  A rich, diverse and complex culture has grown around the country's religious life like a multi-colored vine growing over a stone wall.  Soon, every stone is hidden, but the wall remains, solid and long-lasting.  It may need repair from time to time, but it is a constant beneath the vines that grow, die back, grow again and change color from season to season.

A person seeking to learn about the world's different faiths can enter Hinduism through Vedic philosophy that is the wall under the vine, or through India's culture and rituals that are the vine itself.  Traditional Vedanta is one of India's six philosophical systems and has been interpreted by dozens of respected gurus or teachers.  This chapter focuses primarily on the philosophy and teachings of the Ramakrishna lineage, sometimes referred to as neo-Vedanta, along with the festive atmosphere and rituals commonly found in Hindu temples in America. We will refer to Vedantists when talking about followers of the Ramakrishna and Vivekananda lineage in the West, Hinduism when referring to the religion, and Hindus when talking about people who follow Hindu faith. Many of the terms used are written in Sanskrit, the language of Hindu scriptures (the Vedas) and the classical literary language of India. We'll give you translations in the body of the text and in the glossary that follows.

## A Visitor's View

Think of yourself as a person eager to know about other religions. We have chosen to begin with the sacred space of the five major religions of the world. So a person may think of herself[1] as a visitor to a Center or a Temple to explore the sacred space of this religion. As one seeking the wisdom of the East, she begins her exploration of Hinduism at a worship center that lays bare the timeless insights of India's ancient philosophers with all their paradoxes and brilliance. She then takes this knowledge to a Hindu temple, which provides religious and cultural nourishment to individuals of Indian descent who want to stay connected to their roots.

I remember well my first visit to the Vedanta Center of Atlanta on an Easter Sunday. About thirty people sat on folding chairs in the living room of a small ranch house. A framed drawing of the laughing Christ hung on the wall behind a saffron-robed monk who gave an Easter "sermon" unlike any I had heard before. It was a celebration of the divinity within each of us. There were no glorious choirs to herald Jesus' rising from the tomb, but there was an intimacy and sweetness that permeated the room. Jesus is Truth. But not the only Truth. It was a celebration of all miraculous arisings, from all kinds of deaths.

As someone who had grown up in a Christian family but had followed the Buddhist path for more than twenty years, I felt united with my spiritual past in a new way. The best of both worlds were present that Sunday: the celebration of Easter, reminding me of the Easter Sunday services at the old stone church we used to attend, and the transcendence of mystical religion from the East. Unlike my childhood church experiences, however, this Easter celebration was free of dogma and doctrine. It marked the beginning of my walk along this ancient spiritual path, maintaining and strengthening a meditation practice which had provided me with a strong, spiritual foundation, and introducing me to some of the world's greatest and most ancient scriptures. It is my hope that the reader may be enlightened through my experience and descriptions of this ancient faith.

## American Veda

Hinduism, in comparison to Buddhism, lacks the branding that American Buddhists enjoy, but Hindu or Vedic thought has seeped into American life more than most people realize:  Ralph Waldo Emerson, Dr. Huston Smith, Joseph Campbell, Aldous Huxley, Father Thomas Keating, Anthony de Mello, Eckhart Tolle, and countless others have assimilated Vedic ideas and practices, including meditation.  Many Hindu gurus (teachers) came to America in the second half of the twentieth century.  A couple of them were sufficiently popular that they were featured on the cover of Life and Time magazines.  These gurus, some more reliable and learned than others, introduced thousands of Americans to Vedic philosophy and Hindu scriptures.

## Traditional Hinduism

Traditional or "popular" Hinduism has stayed mostly within the confines of India and the Indian communities who have emigrated to Fiji, Bali, Singapore, Sri Lanka and the U.S.  Like most immigrants, they have a strong desire not only to practice their religion, but to create a space in which they can celebrate their culture and teach their children about their heritage.  Hindu temples in the United States provide a rich cultural experience that can delight and inspire an interested and open-minded Western visitor.  It may require effort to see beyond the multi-armed images, the incense, the flowers, and the bells to the deeply inspiring philosophy that lies at Hinduism's core.  But it is effort well worth exerting.

The oldest and most authoritative scriptures of India are the Vedas.  The Upanishads[2] are the one hundred and eight books representing the philosophical interpretation of the Vedas.  During the more than forty centuries since the Upanishads  were thought to have been written, India has enriched this core philosophy with multiple layers of her diverse culture, in much the same way that Catholicism has amplified Christian devotion with the lives of the saints and embraces certain aspects of the local culture.  Hindus in Bengal honor different gods and goddesses than devotees in other parts of India; in similar fashion, Catholics in Argentina honor different saints than Catholics in Arizona.  Worship of the saints is not a direct analogy to the worship of Hindu gods and goddesses, however, for one important reason.  Hinduism is grounded in polymorphic monism – the belief in one limitless God (Brahman) expressed in an unlimited number of forms.

The Brahman (God) of Hindu or Vedanta philosophy is so far beyond our limited understanding that the only way to have a relationship with It is to see It in Its multiple manifestations. Each "god" or "goddess" therefore represents an attribute of the unknowable, indefinable, eternal God. For example, the god Ganesh is the deity responsible for overcoming obstacles. The goddess Kali represents the female aspect of God and was the deity worshipped by and experienced by Sri Ramakrishna, the saint and mystic whose life inspired the modern Vedanta movement. These deities and many others all reflect the one God, Brahman.

There's a wonderful story about a devout Hindu man who spent his life counting the deities. He recorded in his notebooks hundreds, thousands, millions of names of different deities. Up until the day he died, he was still writing. After he died, his friends eagerly picked up the last book to see how many gods and goddesses he had found. On the last page he had written two words – One God.

## Ramakrishna – An Indian Saint

Like any faith, Hinduism has experienced peaks and valleys of influence. Ramakrishna was part of a renaissance of Hinduism in the late 1800s. Born in rural Bengal, he had little formal education. He did, however, have a life-changing vision when he was six years old. From then on, he studied with the wandering monks and ascetics who passed through his village. As a young man, he moved to Dakshineswar, outside of Calcutta, where he tended to the shrine of Kali.

During his tenure there he had countless ecstatic experiences. He sat in meditation and samadhi[3] for long periods, often at the expense of his official duties; he was intoxicated with the Divine. In time, he attracted many devotees and is now revered as one of India's great saints.

As one monk of the Ramakrishna order describes him: "he linked the old and the new: a product of the centuries of traditional Hinduism, he followed its paths to God-vision; then seeing around him other faiths of the world and that world 'growing small' through modern communication, he practiced the disciplines of Islam and Christianity, reaching the conclusion that all these paths lead to the same summit. He taught the renunciation of ego and harmony of religions."[4]

After Ramakrishna died, his closest disciples formed the Ramakrishna Order which now runs schools, orphanages and hospitals throughout India.

Monks in this tradition, as in all Hindu spiritual lineages, take the title Swami when they have taken their final vows. The Sanskrit word Swami means "he who knows and is the master of himself" or "free from the senses."

Ramakrishna's spiritual heir, Swami Vivekananda, was the first religious teacher to bring Eastern philosophy to America. His first official appearance was at the 1893 Parliament of Religions in Chicago where more than 7,000 people heard his now famous opening statement, "Sisters and brothers of America" It inspired a standing ovation. In his short speech,[5] he quoted from the Bhagavad Gita: "As the different streams having their sources in different places all mingle their water in the sea, so, O Lord, the different paths which men take, through different tendencies, various though they appear, crooked or straight, all lead to Thee!" His message for the West was one of religious harmony, universality and understanding. He founded the Vedanta Centers in America and his books on the four Yogas, compiled from his lectures, are fundamental texts for anyone interested in Vedic spirituality. He spent several years teaching and lecturing in the United States and Europe until his untimely death on July 4, 1902, at the age of thirty-nine.

## Vedanta – A Way to Be Walked

What is Vedanta? In his book Vedanta, The Heart of Hinduism, scholar Hans Torwesten writes: "Vedanta is above all a Way that must be walked. It aims at man's center, his deepest intuition, where the light of truth suddenly shines forth. Its emphasis is on experience and realization." Vedantists believe that the only true proof of the Divine is personal experience. While books and teachers can guide us, we are not to believe until we have that experience for ourselves – the experience of the Divine within. Lalitha Sahasranama, one of the divine texts, says, "Look inward to find the Divine. It is not accessible if you look outward."

Walk into any Vedanta Center, and you are asked to remove your shoes before entering the chapel. This practice is based on Indian culture, but has been adopted by all the Centers as a gesture of respect for a holy space. Inside, you will see rows of chairs facing a simple altar, much like a Christian church. You're unlikely to see any images of Indian gods and goddesses, unless it's one small image in a photo or on the altar. Prominent on the shrine are photographs of Sri Ramakrishna; his wife Sarada Devi, also known as Holy Mother, who led a monastic life with him; and Swami Vivekananda.

102

Christians and Buddhists might be surprised to see representations of Jesus and Buddha on the shrine as well. The Vedanta path honors all great incarnations and saints. An oft-quoted line from one of India's great spiritual texts, the Rig Veda, says: "Truth is one: sages call it by many names." Vedantists and Hindus believe that God has incarnated numerous times and will continue to do so -- Jesus is as welcome on our altar as Krishna, the name God takes in the great Hindu "bible" known as the Bhagavad Gita.

The Om (A-U-M) symbol will be in evidence somewhere, maybe over the shrine. According to the ancient writings of India, Om is the holy sound of God. It is ubiquitous in Hindu art and has found its way into American life, although often in a superficial way. How many of us have attended yoga classes and heard the teacher and students chant Om? Or have seen it on the cover of books about Eastern philosophy, even on T-shirts? An in-depth study of the history and spiritual significance of Om could fill this entire chapter, if not the book, so for now we will leave the mystical chant of Om and continue exploring a typical Vedanta Center.

It's Sunday morning at 11:00 AM. Candles are lit on the altar, alongside vases of fresh flowers. Like any religious space, the Vedanta Center's altar is a focus of reverence. As devotees enter – Westerners and Indians both – they may bow before the altar, or kneel and touch their heads to the ground. Many will offer love and respect to Ramakrishna. Some may open their hearts to Sri Sarada Devi, who continued Ramakrishna's work after he died. Others may honor Vivekananda, Buddha or Jesus. Still others may be non-dualists, focusing on Consciousness, beyond form, beyond personality.

Vedanta philosophy is non-dogmatic and one of the most flexible and open religious systems in the world today. Swami Vivekananda emphasized this and the importance of each religion in a speech he gave in Hartford, Connecticut in March 1895. He said:

*"The messages that are coming down to us from the prophets and holy men and women of all sects and nations are joining their forces and speaking to us with the trumpet voice of the past. And the first message it brings us is: Peace be unto you and to all religions. It is not a message of antagonism, but of one united religion.*

*"At the beginning of this century [the 19th] it was almost feared that religion was at an end. Under the tremendous sledge-hammer blows of scientific research, old superstitions were crumbling away like*

*masses of porcelain. Many thought the case hopeless and the cause
of religion lost once and forever. But the tide has turned and to the
rescue has come - what? The study of comparative religions. By the
study of different religions we find that, in essence, they are one."* [6]

What a wonderful foretaste of today's interfaith movement!

## Lead Us from the Unreal to the Real

Vedanta is not a congregational religion. A Vedantist's spiritual goal is
an individual one - to realize the Consciousness that underlies all of existence
and thereby connect directly with the Divine. There are no prayer books or
hymnals. The lectures and classes are designed to help the individual aspirant
realize the impermanence or "unreality" of the physical world and to reach an
understanding of God or Consciousness as the "ground of being" and God
as immanent in all beings. The body and the mind are both matter which is
"unreal" and belong to the world of appearances. Only Consciousness, that
part of us that is the witness, that exists even when we are in deep sleep, is
real. In any Vedanta Center, a visitor is likely to hear quoted a prayer from the
Brihadaranyaka Upanishad: "Lead us from the Unreal to the Real, from Darkness
unto Light, from Death to Immortality." By fully realizing and embodying this
philosophy -- a journey that will probably take many lifetimes -- a devotee has
the opportunity to reach Moksha or Liberation which can best be described as
realizing what we really are - Divine beings.

Swami Yogeshananda, the spiritual leader of the Vedanta Center of
Atlanta for nearly twenty years, describes Vedanta on the Center's website:
"Vedanta is not a creed, but is, in a sense, the foundation of all creeds and
religions, inasmuch as it offers explanation of the psychological states pertaining
to it, and unfolds the nature of reality in all its aspects. Vedanta does not believe
in conversion, but holds that all the great religions are true and beneficial when
sincerely practiced; for it has discovered that Truth is One, though it is called by
various names and worshiped under different forms.

"Vedanta does not believe in a negative view of life, which stresses the
imperfections and weaknesses of the human being, but emphasizes that we are
really - in our essential nature - pure, perfect, blissful, omniscient, omnipotent
and Divine. It seeks to bring out the Divine perfection in us and to make it bear
on the affairs of everyday life, by prescribing various effective means suitable to

the individual temperaments." [7]

Gaining this knowledge is the life-long struggle for both the Hindu and the Vedantist. On a typical Sunday morning the speaker, probably a monk ordained in the Ramakrishna Order, will offer a carefully-researched lecture on a topic such as: "Concentration and Detachment," "Yoga and Psychotherapy," "Why and How We Meditate," "Joy of Solitude" or "Karma Yoga." He may quote from the Gospel of Sri Ramakrishna and the writings of Swami Vivekananda. He may reference the teachings of other Ramakrishna monks, or the teachings of Jesus or Buddha. He may challenge the visitor's intellect by discussing Vedanta's approach to ethical and philosophical issues. "For every step forward spiritually," says one teacher, "the devotee must take two steps forward ethically."

He may reference Christian mystics and teachers such as Meister Eckhart, the German theologian who preached the presence of God in the individual soul. "A man should be empty of self and all things," Eckhart once wrote, echoing the Vedic belief that each individual is destined to move beyond the ego (the little self) and realize the Divine (the true Self.)

The lecturer will be open to questions. No question will be considered out of line, no thoughtful inquiry heretical. Vivekananda himself was a curious, college-educated, often rebellious young man when he first encountered Ramakrishna, often challenging him. Vedanta devotees are encouraged to adopt this same spirit of inquiry and not accept any idea as dogma. Our own spiritual experiences, primarily through meditation and deep study, lead us to a deeper understanding of the Divine.

Our visitor can be confident that none of the answers given will be designed to convert him. Vedic spirituality, as expressed in both Vedanta Centers and Hindu temples, does not believe in conversion. If a Christian visitor, for example, were to ask any Hindu or Vedantist if she is on the right path, she will be told something like this: "If you have found a path that suits your temperament, and are following it with devotion and single-mindedness, you are sure to reach your spiritual goal." Monks in the Ramakrishna lineage have written books such as "Sermon on the Mount from a Vedantic Perspective," "Emerson and Vedanta," "Hinduism and Christianity." This openness to Christianity reflects one of its key tenets – the acceptance of all religious paths. Many Centers are champions of interfaith dialogue.

## Four Pathways to God

There are four paths to God; each of them is designated as a type of Yoga. Those types are Karma Yoga, Jnana Yoga, Bhakti Yoga, and Raja Yoga. If "Karma Yoga" is the topic for the teachings this particular Sunday, our visitor will learn about the practice of self-realization through work. The Sanskrit word "karma" means action or work. The Bhagavad Gita, (translated as "The Song of God") written between the first and fifth centuries CE, poetically explains this path through the story of the warrior Arjuna, who is faced with a horrible dilemma. After years of fruitless negotiations to end a family feud, Arjuna is going to war against his own relatives. Standing on the battle field, he suddenly loses his courage – how can he kill his own relatives? He calls on his friend Krishna, who appears to him and asks him, do you want all my horses and chariots and weapons, or do you want me to ride on your chariot and be your guide? Wisely Arjuna chooses the latter.

Most of the book is a conversation between Krishna and Arjuna that takes place before the battle. Krishna, whom we soon learn is an incarnation of God, outlines the nature of God and gives Arjuna a recipe for moral, spiritual living. In the end, through Sri Krishna's teachings, he realizes that he cannot kill his cousins – all he will do if he goes into battle is destroy their bodies, not their souls. He also learns that he must fulfill his own "dharma" – sacred duties and responsibilities.

Read literally, the Gita is about a warrior who finally regains his courage to go into battle. Like Jewish Midrash and New Testament stories, however, it is a metaphor for the internal battles we fight between our higher and lower natures. It also reminds us to stay on the battlefield by engaging with life even as we aspire to develop spiritually. One teacher recommends giving all of life "a Godward turn."

The recipe for spiritual life in the Gita is told in terms of the four yogas. In our society, yoga has come to mean a good workout at a yoga studio. Traditionally hatha yoga or the physical poses were just the preparation for meditation. The Sanskrit word yoga means union and yoking. Union of self and the Divine, and yoking like oxen, training the mind. The four different yogas describe four different ways to achieve self-realization or union with God, each according to his or her temperament.

## Karma Yoga -- The Path of Work as Service

With Karma the challenge lies in remaining unattached to the result, whether it's the success of a project, praise from a client, or a raise. Krishna clearly says in the Gita, God is the doer. In other words, "Thy will, not my will, be done." The Gita also admonishes us to follow our own path. It is better to do our own "work" imperfectly than to do another's perfectly.

For example, a friend of mine is a physician at a children's hospital. She spends long days in the operating room treating babies with life-threatening, congenital heart conditions. She adheres to the Hippocratic Oath to save every child. However, over the years it has become clear to her that the end result of surgery is ultimately not in the control of the clinical team. Some children who have a good prognosis die unexpectedly; others with a poor prognosis survive and thrive. As a young doctor, she felt attached to the outcome of her work – the death of any child was devastating, but it was especially confounding when children who were expected to do well, died. At one time my friend even contemplated leaving the medical profession. However, by nurturing a karma yoga attitude toward her work, she now realizes that she can be a competent, deeply committed doctor without being emotionally attached to the results. Vedanta philosophy has helped her become even more engaged on the battlefield of pediatric medicine.

Westerners may be familiar with the word karma in another context: we talk about "good karma" and "bad karma." Karma is the law of cause and effect. If I eat too many cookies (cause), I will gain weight (effect); if I gain weight (cause) I run a greater risk of getting diabetes or heart disease (effect). If I get diabetes (cause) I am a participant in the growing cost of healthcare (effect). If I steal from a friend (cause), I will cause her emotional pain (effect). That pain (cause) will create a rift in our friendship (effect) and so on.

The law of karma is simple to understand but a challenge to incorporate into one's life. But how mindful we become when we examine our actions from the point of view of the harm they may inflict on ourselves and others, not just in this lifetime but many lifetimes! Our visitor will hear little talk about sin, however. Instead she will hear us talk of ignorance, of moving from lower truth to higher truth.

Good karma follows a similar pattern. Our actions in previous lifetimes impact our experiences in this lifetime, while our actions in this lifetime may not show their effect until a future lifetime. In this way, karma and reincarnation are inextricably linked. The philosophy of karma brings with it an enormous sense of personal responsibility.

## Jnana Yoga -- The Path of Discrimination

Another way to self-realization is the Jnana path, or the path of discrimination. Jnana means knowledge. Through reason and self-inquiry you find your way to Brahman.

The jnana path is closely linked with Advaita Vedanta. Advaita means "not two" – God is one, everything is divine, there is nothing that is not God. This is the razor-sharp path of non-dualism which Vivekananda introduced to his Western disciples. Everything that is not Brahman is merely illusion or maya. Thousands of pages have been written about the Advaita philosophy, one of the most intellectually challenging and fascinating paths of Vedic spirituality. The greatest proponent of Advaita Vedanta philosophy was Shankaracharya or "Shankara The Teacher," who lived in ninth-century India.

A spiritual seeker following this path will study holy texts, but his curiosity and thirst for knowledge will not end there. He will commit to intensive self-inquiry. Who am I? What is Real? What is God? He will learn to discriminate between what is "Real" (Brahman) and what is not Real (the physical world, including his body, mind and Ego). In time, he will come full circle to realize that since all of creation is a manifestation of Brahman (God), everything in it is Brahman. Everything therefore is Real. Everything is Consciousness. As T.S. Eliot wrote in *Four Quartets*, "We shall not cease from exploration, and the end of all our exploring will be to arrive where we started and know the place for the first time."

Vedanta encompasses science comfortably because it teaches that everything is ultimately part of God, or God manifest in different forms. The "aha" moments that scientists experience at the moment of discovery are moments that we can all experience in our own way. These states of realized concentration are called Samadhi. Vedic spirituality teaches that there are many different levels of Samadhi and that every person is destined to experience all of them, if not in this life, then in a future life. Saints and mystics in all faith traditions reach exquisite levels of Samadhi when they are in deep meditation or experiencing visions of the Divine.

All Vedantists are cautioned to suspend belief until they have experienced what is being taught. When faith is blind, it can lead to fundamentalism or other perversions. When faith is reasoned, and based on personal, empirical evidence, it becomes a rock on which to build a spiritual life. This rational approach may be why many scientists, doctors and intellectuals are drawn to Vedanta. The author and thinker Aldous Huxley recommended to a young Huston Smith, who was on his way to St. Louis, that he visit Swami Satprakashananda there. "I'm not sure I knew what the word swami meant at the time," Smith said later, "but of course I held Huxley in such high regard that the first week I was there I looked up Swami Satprakashananda and visited him." Smith adds, "I returned home with a copy of the Katha Upanishad under my arm, and before I went to bed I opened it. By the second page I was glued to it and said, 'This is it!'" [8]

## Bhakti -- The Path of Devotion

The path of Bhakti is the path of Love. Bhakti devotees may worship an incarnation such as Jesus or Krishna. They may meditate on the image of Sri Ramakrishna whom Vedanta devotees also consider an incarnation. Unlike the limitless Brahman, which has no attributes, the God that one worships as a Bhakta is the God with attributes, or the ishwara. The Bhakti path is sometimes seen as less demanding than the other yogas, particularly Jnana yoga, but it is far from easy. To love without expecting anything in return; to love in good times and bad; to love those people whose personalities we do not like – these and other challenges meet us on this path. Through daily meditation and the practice of love, however, bhakti practitioners come to realize the divinity of their chosen ideal or ishwara. In time, they realize their own divinity and that of all beings. Swami Satprakashananda, founder of the Vedanta Center of St. Louis, wrote: "As love intensifies, the devotee's individual self becomes so completely unified with God that he realizes the divine being as his very Self, and as the Self in all beings." In this way the Bhakti path and Jnana path end up in the same place – the realization that the Divine, God, is in everything.

If our visitor is Jewish or Christian, she will likely feel quite familiar with this path. It mirrors the Judeo-Christian ideal of loving one's neighbor as oneself described in Leviticus 19:18, 19:34 and in the Gospel of Mark 12:30-31 "Do not seek revenge or bear a grudge against anyone among your people, but love your neighbor as yourself. I am the LORD....The foreigner residing among you must be treated as your native-born. Love them as yourself, for you were foreigners in Egypt. I am the LORD your God." (Leviticus). In Mark, when asked which was the most important commandment, Jesus says: "Love the Lord your God

**109**

with all your heart, and with all your soul, and with all your mind, and with all your strength. The second is this: Love your neighbor as yourself. There is no commandment greater than these."

All Vedanta Centers set aside a time at least twice a day for the monks to care for the shrine. The monk honors the four elements by lighting a candle (fire), burning incense (earth), ringing a bell or waving a fan (air), and pouring water into sacred vessels. This ritual reminds the practitioner that God is immanent in the shrine. When devotees attend the meditation ceremony, perhaps once a day, they sit in silence, saying a mantra or holy word silently to themselves, perhaps using prayer beads to help them focus on their divine ideal or ishwara.

## Raja Yoga -- the Path of Meditation

Meditation is the fourth and final path that encompasses the other three. Known as Raja or Royal yoga, it is the spiritual practice that every follower of Hinduism or Vedic spirituality embraces. It is through meditation that we can calm the mind, witness our Ego and the games it plays with us, and access the Divine presence within us.

The beauty of Vedanta is its flexibility and openness. Without falling into relativism, Vedanta allows the devotee freedom to meditate on whichever Divinity he chooses. Many meditate on Ramakrishna; others meditate on Jesus, Buddha or simply Truth. How beautiful it is to sit silently in a room for thirty minutes with other devotees, each immersed in his or her own meditation. When the incense has burned to dust, and the candles are snuffed out, one feels a greater calm and a renewed connection with fellow devotees, even if no one has spoken a word. And our visitor will be welcomed to meditate with us.

Once a devotee has learned to meditate, usually from the monk who runs the Center, she is encouraged to create a space at home for meditation. This practice brings God into the home, in much the same way as when grace is said before a home-cooked meal. The discipline of taking half an hour, twice a day, to meditate is a challenge for most of us who work forty hours a week and care for our families. But meditation requires that we take a break from the busy-ness of our daily activities and spend time with the Lord or contemplating Truth or Consciousness. Of course, the duties of a householder are not to be neglected, but taking time to nurture the Divine within us is not to be taken lightly. Meditating daily develops the psychic muscles required for deep connection with Reality, the same way lifting weights daily develops the physical muscles. Both require commitment and consistency in order to see results.

In meditation the Vedantist or Hindu may have a vision that is indescribable in words, she may glimpse what she can only describe as Consciousness, or she may repeat the mantra hundreds of times over hundreds of days and never feel she has progressed. Over time, however, a devotee falls in love with God. One only has to remember the posthumous writings of Mother Teresa in which she tells of her own darkness, to realize that every aspirant, however dedicated to God, struggles with realization.

## Studying the Scriptures

If our visitor returns to the Vedanta Center on certain weeknights, she will be able to sit in on a class that is studying the Vedantic scriptures. Whether we are studying the Gospel of Sri Ramakrishna, written by a devotee known as M, or the writings of Vivekananda, whose voice rings with strength and reason, there is plenty of time for inquiry and questions. Some monks are disappointed if no questions are asked!

One of the ideas that Vivekananda espoused and brought to the West was that "by the Vedas no books are meant." What does he mean, when we have discussed all along the importance of the Upanishads to Vedic thought? Simply that knowledge is always evolving and that "Vedanta," which means "the end of knowledge," refers to the cusp on which we find ourselves when scientific discoveries change our world view in both subtle and dramatic ways. Imagine the shift in people's religious outlook when Galileo went public with his discovery that the sun, not the earth, was the center of the universe. It landed him in hot water with philosophers and clerics who charged him with heresy. Fear, denial and ignorance are always the enemies of Truth, whether in our own or in another time.

By now, our visitor may be aching to sing a hymn or chant a prayer. There is some of that too at our Vedanta Center, but the Vedantic path is not traditionally congregational. That is not to say that Vedanta communities are not strongly connected. The sincere search for Truth requires community support as well as individual effort, and of course the wisdom and guidance of a good teacher. For example, we need the insights of others regarding the issue of evil. What is it? How do we explain it?

**111**

## Hindu View of Evil

People may ask, if science and everything we know in the Universe is God, what about evil? Vedic philosophy takes a position that may seem puzzling to people grounded in one of the Abrahamic faiths. Vedantists believe that good and evil will always exist in this physical world. The scales are always balanced between them. Without evil, how would we know good?

By now, our visitor is probably in deep philosophical conversation with one of our community members who will remind her of Isaiah 45:7 where Jehovah says, "I send forth good, I send forth evil." If God is everything, then God also encompasses what we call evil. And yet God as Brahman is beyond both good and evil because It[9] has no attributes, one of the many paradoxes that lie on the Vedic path.

Evil, from a Vedantic or Hindu standpoint, can also mean ignorance or lack of knowledge about our true, Divine nature. This is only a partial response to the question of evil, but a full exploration of the issue reaches beyond the intent of this brief writing.

## The Monks

The Ramakrishna monks who head up the more than twenty Vedanta Centers in the United States are primarily teachers and rarely officiate at baptisms or weddings. Sometimes devotees are disappointed by this, wanting to mark an important rite of passage with a religious ritual. The monks may offer blessings and attend a wedding at a church or a home, but they do not officiate on these occasions.

Ramakrishna monks devote their lives to teaching a philosophy that is open, reasonable and non-dogmatic. If our visitor sat down with a monk and asked about life and God, the word Consciousness would come up sooner rather than later. Consciousness is God and God, or Brahman, is Consciousness. Brahman is God without attributes, unknowable, immutable, indefinable, impersonal, eternal. God is the ground of being. In this way Brahman is closest to the Jewish Yahweh. This monk will also tell him about the Personal God, Ishwara, the God with attributes.

Lastly, our teacher monk will encourage the visitor to see the Divine in himself and in all things, known as the Atman. Individual soul, or Atman, is part of the Divine Soul or Universal Soul, like the waves that are part of the ocean.

A person who through experience realizes this is freed from the bonds of the world.

This is where Vedic teachings become templates for interfaith thought and conversation. If all beings are Divine, grounded in the same Consciousness, then any disagreements between faiths are only superficial, having more to do with form than substance. Vivekananda hoped the time would come when each person had her own religion, meaning that each person has a direct path to God.

## What Vedanta Means to Me

Vedanta has given me ballast and depth on my spiritual journey. Ramakrishna's deep visionary experiences in samadhi are balanced by the rational and intellectual teachings of Vivekananda. Both are true, both are honored. And Holy Mother represents the feminine, something sorely lacking in my religious upbringing. Vedanta sets out a clear path, according to my temperament. It has also shown me that I can – and should – ask questions. Healthy skepticism is encouraged. Vedanta has helped me understand religion as both an art and a science, to be studied and practiced daily. And most of all, it teaches me to see the Divine in every person I meet, in every situation I encounter, in every joy and every grief. It's not an easy path for me, and I regularly forget that every person is Divine, especially those whose personalities I don't enjoy. But as one of my teachers says, the "pleasant" path in life is easy. Moving to the "good" is what each of us must do on this spiritual path. I remain deeply committed because Vedanta challenges me intellectually, offers me multiple ways to walk the path, and does not negate any part of life. Vedanta gives me practical knowledge that teaches me how to experience the Divine directly.

## Hindu Sacred Space

Leaving the Vedanta Center for now, our visitor heads across town to the Hindu temple. It is a sensory experience quite unlike the Vedanta Center. She will hear bells and chanting. She will smell incense and flowers. She will see intricate stone carvings on the walls. She will be dazzled by the dozen or more sculptures of gods and goddesses, many with four, six or eight arms, in clothes of brilliant orange and red. She will see women in saris of all colors, and men and women sitting on the floor reading or chanting. While some temples have chairs, most devotees stand or sit on the floor. This is part of Indian culture. Our visitor will be welcomed with smiles and nods and will be free to stay as long as she likes.

Like most first-generation immigrants, Indian families form strong communities, worship in their own faith and look for ways to preserve their culture for future generations. Hindu temples in the U.S. are therefore replicas of temples in India, in the same way that Christian churches to this day are often inspired by the architecture of Europe's Gothic cathedrals. Imagine, as you drive up to this Hindu temple, a dazzling white stone exterior decorated with sculptures of male and female deities, each representing an attribute of the one God. Seen from above, the plan of the temple closely resembles the plan of a human body in which the Sanctum Sanctorum (garbha gudi) is the head and the outer gate is the lower limb. The spine (gopuram) on the outer gate is the foot of the Lord. Architects, stone masons and sculptors were brought from India to design and build this beautiful temple. It most likely includes a dining hall and kitchen, an auditorium, a space for children's education including traditional music and dance and, of course, plenty of parking. Like most religious communities, Hindu temples foster an environment where their children are safe and their cultural values honored. And like most people of faith, these Indian families rely upon their community's generosity to make their vision of a temple a reality.

The temple will likely be independently run and not affiliated with any political body. Hindus do not look to any organized body to lay down a doctrine or moral guidelines, which is not to say there are no moral teachings. They look to the Vedas and the teachings of their great epics for moral guidance.

## Many Images, One God

Our visitor will see rows of shoes outside the door of the temple. She too will slip off her shoes as a gesture of respect before entering. Inside, the atmosphere is warm and festive, and the myths and symbolism of Indian culture are evident in the shrines that line the walls. The deities depicted are worshipped much as a Catholic prays to the different saints. Unlike the saints, however, each statue here represents an attribute of God. Our visitor may be tempted to think of each statue as a separate god, but the devotees there will gently correct her. For if God is limitless, representations of divine attributes are limitless too. This is polymorphic monism.

Let's study one statue so we can better understand what it means to the Hindu devotee. We find Goddess Durga in the first alcove. Under the colorful

114

clothes and fresh garlands of flowers, her skin is black, containing all the colors of the universe. Her eyes are large and wide, reminding devotees that not only are we observing her, but God, as Durga, is seeing us. She is the mother of the universe and believed to be the power behind the creation, preservation, and destruction of the world. Since time immemorial she has been worshipped as the supreme power of the Supreme Being and has been mentioned in many scriptures. Like many Indian deities, she is shown with multiple arms. In centuries past, this taught devotees that the statue represented God, not a human. It was a teaching tool, much the way stained glass windows in medieval times told Bible stories for those who couldn't read. The multiple arms also are a way of showing which of God's limitless attributes Durga represents.

In one hand, she holds a conch shell which represents God in the form of sound. In another, she holds a bow and arrows, indicating her control over both potential and kinetic energy. She holds a thunderbolt to signify firmness – the devotee of Durga must be firm in one's convictions. Like the thunderbolt that can break anything against which it strikes, without being affected itself, the devotee needs to attack life's challenges without losing faith. The lotus blossom in another hand symbolizes certainty of success in the evolution of spirituality. She holds a discus, a weapon that can destroy wrong-doing and produce an environment conducive to the growth of righteousness, a sword to symbolize knowledge, and a trident indicating that she is the remover of physical, mental and spiritual misery. These symbols are not an end unto themselves, but a gateway to realizing God.

In the West, mythology, philosophy and religion parted ways many centuries ago. In India they are still intertwined. For instance, Hanuman is a figure from the Ramayana, an Indian epic known by every Hindu man, woman and child. It tells the story of Rama, who is worshipped by many Hindus as an incarnation of God. His life is a glorious mix of myth and history, replete with moral lessons. His most loyal companion is Hanuman, who sticks by him through countless dangers and moral challenges. For this reason, he is worshipped in Hindu temples as the perfect devotee.

Westerners may contend that Hunaman, known as the Monkey God, is no more real than a unicorn[10] – a mythical figure with no religious validity. But Hindu worshippers are unimpressed by such distinctions between myth and religion, and many are deeply inspired by this popular image. Our visitor may see worshippers walking around the Hunaman shrine as many as a hundred and eight times, representing the hundred and eight books of the Upanishads. This ritual is an important part of some devotees' visit to their Hindu temple and is known as Pradakshina or circumambulation. The purpose is to concentrate on the Divine, pray and meditate. It is the time one sets aside to focus on prayer and not on extraneous things.

To the Hindu these beautiful sculptures represent the Divine in much the same way as a Christian cross or a Jewish Torah. It is not the physical thing we connect with, but what it symbolizes. Think of a favorite holy text, dog-eared from use, given to us by our grandmother. As much as we treasure this book, it is only a guide; the words are only symbols of the Truth within. Christians do not worship the physical cross; they recognize it as a symbol of Jesus' crucifixion and resurrection. Similarly, Hindus do not worship the sculptures of the deities, but the qualities of God that each represents. They serve as the meeting point, the intersection between the seeker and the Divine.

## The Vedas – Bedrock of Hindu Life

If the Constitution is the bedrock of American secular life, the Vedas are the bedrock of Indian religious life. Americans may refer to the Constitution and quote its most memorable passages, but few of us have read or studied it. It is the same with Hindus and the Vedas.

The Vedas and the Upanishads, however, are the ever-present backdrop of Hindu life. Certain stories from the Vedas are told again and again, but the ordinary Hindu may never have read or studied the Vedas themselves. He will be more familiar with great mythological epics like the Mahabarata, of which the Bhagavad Gita is a part, and the Ramayana. Characters from the Ramayana are popular in Indian life because they teach moral lessons. Where myth ends and faith begins around these epics only the individual devotee can say.

At the Hindu temple, no hymnals or prayer books are in the worship space, although we might see devotees sitting on the floor quietly reading their own spiritual book. In one corner, you might see a family sitting with their newborn child while a priest, his arms and chest bare, gives the baby a blessing. Naming of the baby in a religious ceremony is the first occasion for the family to bring the newborn to the temple. It is a joyous occasion and one can see the happiness in the faces of the parents, grandparents and other members of the extended family and friends.

## Receiving the Priest's Blessings

While revered Swamis may visit a Hindu temple occasionally to give in-depth teachings, weekly sermons are not a component of the Hindu's religious life. This is in part because traditional Hindu families place greater importance on keeping and tending a shrine in their home and daily practicing their worship. They pray and meditate at their personal shrine, and mark religious festivals with the offering of flowers. When they do go to the temple, devotees look forward to receiving darshan. Their visit is incomplete without darshan and prasada in the same way that for many Christians a visit to church is incomplete without holy communion. Both are highly symbolic and filled with meaning, mystery and joy.

Darshan, which means "to be in the presence of the Divine," is given several times a day. As the designated time approaches, devotees form a line in front of a pair of heavy wooden doors. Imagine standing shoulder to shoulder with other devotees as the doors open and the priests emerge from the sacred shrine beyond.

The priests conduct the liturgy and offer blessings. These will include the sacred lighted lamp (called Deepam), lighted camphor (Harathi) with its exotic fragrance, and an offering of food and fruits (Naivedyam). The priest gives devotees sanctified water called tirtham, and Prasadam, a food item, often fruit or nuts, that has been blessed.

The Hindu priest says in Sanskrit: "May the blessings of the Lord prevent untimely death, heal all ailments, this sacred and auspicious water or fruit or juice from the feet of the Lord." The devotees respond "Maha Prasadam," which roughly translates as "honored to receive this blessed offering." It is a moment of reflection, introspection and meditation.

This is the equivalent of benediction as found in the Hebrew Bible in the Book of Numbers: "The Lord bless you and keep you; the Lord make his face to shine upon you and be gracious to you; the Lord lift up his countenance upon you and give you peace. So shall they put my name upon the people of Israel, and I will bless them." (Numbers 6:24-27)

The burning of incense is another act of devotion in the Hindu temple. It is called Dhoopam and is part of any Pooja (celebration) or prayer. I imagine our visitor lighting a stick of incense and leaving it in front of one of the shrines, honoring the one God that is present there as the divine is present in every sacred community.

The priests in a traditional Hindu temple are functionaries; they do not counsel devotees, give sermons or offer spiritual guidance. Instead they tend to the shrine, sing sacred chants, offer Prasad to the devotees, and conduct ceremonies for baptisms or other rites of passage. They are usually trained in India, hired by the American temple and often live on the temple grounds. They may marry and have a family.

## A Hindu Festival

No faith tradition would be complete without rituals and celebrations that mark auspicious days on the religious calendar. And while the Vedanta Center marks a few important feast days during the year, including the holy days of Ramakrishna, Vivekananda and Holy Mother, as well as the birth of Christ and Buddha, nothing compares with the many joyous festivals celebrated by traditional Hindus. It's embedded in their culture. One of the most popular, and most recognized the world over, is Diwali, the Festival of Lights that takes place in the fall and celebrates the triumph of Good over Evil, or Knowledge over Ignorance.

Diwali celebrations involve fireworks, which makes it popular with children. The fireworks start about a month before the actual day and continue for a few days afterwards. It is a festival in which the whole family can participate. In some parts of India, it is also the beginning of the New Year. The day before Diwali is celebrated as Naraka Chaturdasi. Legend has it that Krishna's wife Satyabhama accompanies him in a battle against the demon king, Naraka. When Krishna is rendered unconscious by Naraka, Satyabhama steps in and slays the demon. The whole world celebrates with a festival of lights, and fireworks.

Legend also says that Sri Rama killed Ravana, the ten-headed demon king, at this time. The slaying of Ravana is a metaphor for the fall of Ego. The ten heads of Ravana are our Ego. When one head is cut off, another springs up, and that continues because it is practically impossible for us to conquer our Ego. A person who conquers Ego will be on a path to self realization. Diwali doesn't involve much somber religious observance, but it is a wonderful window through which to glimpse Indian culture that our visitor can enjoy.

Perhaps our visitor will celebrate Diwali one day, or study the writings of Vivekananda and the Advaita philosophers. But for now, with his incense stick still burning in the temple, and his mind on fire with the universal principles of the Vedas, he returns to his own sacred community giving thanks for the beauty of diversity and the Divine joy that is expressed through every faith.

**118**

## Epilogue

Followers of the Abrahamic faiths often find Hinduism to be the most challenging religion to understand. It is complex and highly decentralized, and its core beliefs are superimposed with centuries of Indian culture, myth and ritual. But look beyond the externals, and you will discover a timeless philosophy that encompasses the core tenets of most faiths. One God, limitless and eternal. Practical paths to experience the Divine – meditation and contemplative prayer are direct borrowings from Hinduism and Vedanta. Guidance in living an ethical life and reaching out to others in love and compassion. Hinduism and Vedanta are perhaps unique in their complete acceptance of all religions, but we are blessed to live in a time when many people of faith are reaching across religious divides more than ever before. "Whatever path people travel is My path," says Krishna in the Bhagavad Gita. "No matter where they walk, it leads to Me."

# Notes

1. Since no gender-neutral pronoun exists in the English language, "he," "she," "her," and "his" are used interchangeably in this chapter.
2. Upanishads – see glossary for definition
3. Samadhi is a non-dualistic state of consciousness in which the consciousness of the meditator becomes one with the object of meditation.
4. Swami Yogeshananda, from www.vedanta-atlanta.org
5. From September 11, 2010, through May 1, 2011, the Art Institute of Chicago presented an exhibition, Public Notice 3, by contemporary Indian artist Jitish Kallat. In this site-specific installation, Kallat converted the text of Vivekananda's historic speech to LED displays on each of the 118 risers of the historic Woman's Board Grand Staircase of the Art Institute of Chicago, adjacent to the site of Vivekananda's original address.
6. From "Soul, God and Religion," published in the Complete Works of Swami Vivekananda, Vol. I, Lectures and Discourses; available online at http://www.ramakrishnavivekananda.info/vivekananda/complete_works.htm
7. www.vedanta-atlanta.org
8. From The Way Things Are: Conversations with Huston Smith on the Spiritual Life, edited and with a preface by Phil Cousineau, University of California Press, 2003.
9. We use "It" here because God as Brahman is without attributes and therefore beyond gender. The personal God or ishwara has attributes, including gender, and is described and worshipped in a limitless number of ways.
10. Greek writers of natural history were convinced of the reality of the unicorn, which, in a curious twist, they located in India, a distant and fabulous realm for them.

# Glossary

**Advaita** – Literally "not-two," non-duality; school of Vedanta according to which there is only one reality – the Brahman – and all multiplicity merely illusion (maya).#

**Arjuna** – Hero of the "Bhagavad Gita" to whom Krishna (as God incarnate) reveals his wisdom teachings.

**Atman** – The indestructible real Self behind the superficial personality.#

**Bhagavad Gita** – "Song of the Lord"; a short book in verse embodying the principles of the religious life as espoused by later Hinduism.#

**Bhakti** – Loving devotion; worship of the personal god (in whatever manifestation)#

**Brahman** – The Absolute; the Supreme Reality of Vedanta philosophy.*

**Darshan** – A vision, or glimpse, as in a vision of the Divine. Also, being in the presence of the Divine. Devotees receive darshana in the temple as an act of devotion.

**Durga** – One of the names of the Mother Goddess.#

**Guru** – Spiritual teacher.#

**Hanuman** – Hanuman, the mighty ape that aided Lord Rama in his expedition against evil forces in the Hindu epic "Ramayana," is one of the most popular Hindu deities. He is worshiped as a symbol of physical strength, perseverance and devotion.

**Ishwara** – The personal God.*

**Jnana** – Knowledge of God arrived at through reasoning and discrimination; also denotes the process of reasoning by which the Ultimate Truth is attained. The word is generally used to denote the knowledge by which one is aware of one's identity with Brahman.*

**Karma** – Action in general; duty; law of cause and effect

**Karma yoga** – (lit. union with God through action.) The path by which the aspirant seeks to realize God through work without attachment.*

**Krishna** – An incarnation of God, whose wisdom teachings are the core of the "Bhagavad Gita."

**Mantra** – Holy Sanskrit text; word or phrase used in meditation.

**Maya** – A term of Vedanta philosophy denoting ignorance obscuring the vision of God; the Cosmic Illusion on account of which the One appears as many, the Absolute as the Relative; it is also used to denote binding attachment.*

**Prasad** – Food or drink that has been offered to the Deity. It is regarded as possessing spiritual merit.*

**Pradakshina** – Circumambulation. Walking around the image of a deity as an act of devotion.

**Pooja** – Ritualistic worship.* Usually associated with the Bhakti or devotional path.

**Ramakrishna** – An Indian saint and mystic (1836-1886). He practiced the disciplines of Islam and Christianity, and through his transcendental experience reached the conclusion that these paths all lead to the same summit. He taught the renunciation of ego and the harmony of religions. His followers founded the Ramakrishna Mission and Order in India and the Vedanta Societies in the United States and around the world.

**Rishi** – Seer, sage.

**Samadhi** – State of deep absorption; rapture.# Ecstasy, trance, communion with God.*

**Sanatana Dharma** – Lit. "eternal religion"; the expression Hindus traditionally use when referring to their religion.

**Sarada Devi** – Sri Ramakrishna's wife who lived a monastic life with him and was his first disciple. A great saint in her own right, she is also known as Holy Mother. She continued Ramakrishna's work for many years after he died.

**Upanishads** – Collective name for the 108 books representing various philosophical interpretations of the Vedas, particularly the later ones (900-500 BCE).

**Vedas** – The most sacred scriptures of the Hindus.* Earliest known hymns, prayers, ritual texts, and philosophical treatises of India.#

**Vivekananda** – (1863-1902) – Iconoclast, skeptic, college-educated disciple of Sri Ramakrishna, he gave sensational talks at the Parliament of Religions at the 1893 World's Fair in Chicago. In 1899, he founded, with brother disciples, the Ramakrishna Order and Mission of India and the Vedanta Societies in the United States and Europe.

**Yoga** – Union of the individual soul and the Universal Soul; also the method by which to realize this union.*


# -- definitions courtesy of *Vedanta: Heart of Hinduism* by Hans Torwesten
* -- definitions courtesy of *The Gospel of Ramakrishna*, Abridged Edition, translated into English with an Introduction by Swami Nikhilananda

# For Further Reading

Harshananda, Swami. *Hindu Gods and Goddesses* (a full explanation of the rationale behind the many aspects of God, with illustrations). Vedanta Press.

Nikhilananda, Swami, trans. *The Gospel of Ramakrishna*. Ramakrishna-Vivekananda Center.

Prabhavananda, Swami. *The Sermon on the Mount According to Vedanta*. Vedanta Press.

Prabhavananda, Swami and Isherwood, Christopher, translators. *The Bhagavad Gita: The Song of God with introduction by Aldous Huxley*. Vedanta Press.

Prabhavananda, Swami and Manchester, Frederick, translators. *The Upanishads: Breath of the Eternal*. Vedanta Press.

Torwesten, Hans. *Vedanta: Heart of Hinduism*. Grove Press.

Vrajaprana, Pravrajika. *Vedanta: A Simple Introduction*. Vedanta Press.

**Online:**

*Complete Works of Vivekananda*
http://www.ramakrishnavivekananda.info/vivekananda/complete_works.htm
Vedanta Society of Southern California, www.vedanta.org
Vedanta Center of Atlanta, www.vedanta-atlanta.org

*Buddist Sacred Space*

# CHAPTER FIVE

# The Center: Sacred Space of Soto Zen Buddhists

------------

## Gareth Young

**"Hi, and welcome to the Atlanta Soto Zen Center.** I'm Gareth; are you here for Newcomers Instruction?"

"Hi, I'm Sophie." The young woman, likely in her early twenties, extends her right hand to meet mine. She looks me straight in the eyes as she says, "Yes, I'm here for Newcomers," then glances around with bright eyes and obvious curiosity.

"Great," I say. "We'll be sitting down in this room off to the side, but first would you mind putting your shoes on the shelf in here?"

Sophie smiles and follows me into the library behind the vestibule to slip off her shoes.

Most Sunday mornings and Wednesday evenings we have visitors like Sophie – individuals, married couples, parent and child – and occasionally we have larger numbers, and even organized groups from schools or other religious organizations. When they enter our vestibule, visitors are often nervous and unsure of themselves, and we try very hard to be welcoming and make them feel at home, for almost all of our members were, like Sophie, raised in another faith tradition, and we remember our own "first visit" to the Zen Center. My own story contains many elements common to most of our members.

I was raised in the United Kingdom under the umbrella of the Church of England. Though I was never a regular churchgoer, Christianity pervaded my social and educational environment during my early life. In my thirties I began to develop a nagging doubt about the purpose of life and of my daily actions, and when the Christianity of my earlier years did not help me in the way I needed, I did not know what to do. So I turned where I had been trained to go in times of need: I went to a bookstore.

It was not long before my extensive reading led me to develop an interest in meditation in general. As I went deeper, my curiosity became directed in particular to the form of meditation manifested in Zen Buddhism. But although Zen meditation (or "zazen") made great intellectual sense to me, it took some time before I overcame the preconception from my Christian background that meditation is some kind of mind-emptying, trance-inducing dangerous ritual. When I started to practice, though, I soon found myself engaged in an intermittent but deeply rewarding home-based and private individual practice. I continued this practice for some time. I knew in my heart that there was much more to this practice that I could not find alone and that I needed to join a community, but I bore great anxiety about visiting a zendo or Zen Center, fearing that to do so would expose me to strange practices and perhaps a bizarre cult.

As my home practice developed, however, I gradually came to realize that I needed a teacher and a community, so I swallowed deeply and drove to the Zen Center, where the apparent austerity of a dark décor and climate of silence intimidated me and appeared to validate my concerns. Though intellectually I recognized that these existed to support a contemplative practice, it was with considerable trepidation when for the first time I stepped into the meditation hall and sat facing the wall.

Some visitors report that they immediately feel as if they have "come home," but many retain a feeling of awkwardness for some time. For me it took several visits and a number of conversations after services with members to begin feeling at one with their simple humanity. Even when I felt completely at home, for a while I was still uncomfortable discussing my practice with my friends, family, and work colleagues.

"So let's go in and sit down, Sophie."

We walk back through the vestibule to a small room that is roughly twelve by twelve feet square with meditation seats on three sides and an altar and meditation mat for the instructor on the fourth. I take my position on the instructor's seat, instinctively folding my legs, and saying, "Don't worry about 'sitting right'; just make yourself comfortable and let's chat. Mostly we're going to talk about how to meditate, but we'll also talk a little about our practice at this center, and what to expect in terms of protocols, services and the like.

First, though, I want to make sure that I direct this conversation to your own experience and questions, so let me ask you: do you have experience meditating, or is there anything in particular you'd like to find out about the subject?"

Sophie sits down and puts her purse on the floor under the bench, looks around the room, and says, "I've read about meditation and it sounds pretty cool; I think it would help me to relax. I'm doing a PhD at Georgia Tech, and it's very stressful."

"What are you studying?"

We have a short chat during which I discover that Sophie is working on the cutting edge of some form of computer chip technology that is fascinating but way beyond me, and occasionally I glance through the open door into the vestibule as people arrive, exchanging silent greetings with many friends and regulars. An unfamiliar face appears and looks around, so I say, "Excuse me just a minute, Sophie," and call out, "Hi, are you here for Newcomers?"

The gentleman, probably in his fifties, looks at me with a relieved expression. "Yes, I am."

"Excellent. If you'd step through into the next room and put your shoes on the shelf, then come and join us in here, that'd be great."

He returns sock-footed, and as he makes himself comfortable I introduce Sophie and me, and the new arrival introduces himself as Simon. I ask about his meditation experience and whether he has any questions.

"Well," Simon says, "I've been meditating occasionally at home for three or four years, and I've read about every book on Buddhism and meditation under the sun, and I just figured if I were really going to do this thing then I should come to a Zen Center. I did a Google search, and there you were...and, well, here I am."

"Welcome again. And any questions?"

"Oh, yes. As I said, I've read a lot, but one thing is still not really clear to me: is Buddhism a philosophy or a religion?"

I laugh. "That's a really good question. As I told Sophie, we're going to spend most of our time together talking about how we meditate." I look at the clock beside me and say, "It's a little after nine o'clock; I assume no one else is going to come today, so let's start with your question, Simon."

The relaxed timing, the open door, and the casual conversations are typical of our informal—though serious—practice. Our members and teachers (with the sole exception of our Abbot) are laity with jobs, families, and homes, and we often joke about our practice as being "Guerilla Zen," something we can only have by allowing ourselves to rush in out of the mayhem of our everyday lives and steal a few moments of zazen. Not only do we believe this approach makes Zen more accessible to all, but it is also the only form of practice that can work for our membership.

"Reading about Zen is a great place to start," I tell Simon, "but it can never get at the truth, which can only come out of practice. We all need teachings, whether books or mentors or guides, but we need to recognize that the teachings are just fingers pointing at the moon, and not the moon itself. Buddhism has many devoted followers around the globe who attend services, practice devotions, and the like. It has a great diversity of services and practices around which communities cohere and organize. It has establishments and authorizing bodies. In this sense you can certainly see it as a religion.

"On the other hand, during the last two and a half thousand years, vast volumes of books have been written about Buddhism, both as a guide to practice and as a commentary on it. There is a massive library of philosophical teachings, and in as much as these describe a way of viewing the world, an analysis of how and why Zen works, and so forth, then certainly you can see Buddhism as a philosophy.

"But for us, these are only partial truths. Have you ever heard phrases like, 'If you see the Buddha on the road, kill the Buddha,' or, 'If you say the word Buddha, then spit'?"

Simon nods. "Yeah, but it always seemed kind of weird."

I smile. "It does, doesn't it? But think about it this way. Buddha didn't intend to form a religion or a philosophy. He simply found a practice that helped him see the Truth, see the way things really are. And he didn't preach about what this truth is, but about the personal, practical path that each of us can follow to uncover it for ourselves. He tried to explain to people who were around him that this insight was possible for each of us, and that it was up to us to discover it for ourselves. Sure, we need community and teachers and the structure of teachings to guide us, but ultimately it's our responsibility. In this sense Buddhism is actually neither a philosophy nor a religion, but a personal practice. Once the truth of Buddhism is realized, then the practitioner has no more use for Buddhism, because it's just another label."

"So I have a question," Sophie says. "Who was this Buddha person, and how did his teaching come to Atlanta?"

I smile again. "That is kind of where this takes us, isn't it? Let me tell you a story."

## A Brief History of Zen Buddhism

"The root Sanskrit word buddh, from which the Buddha is given his name, means 'to wake up,' and Buddha therefore simply means, 'one who has woken up.' When we talk of Buddha, though, we usually mean one person born in ancient India, and giving him this name is a testament to his actual experience, and to the experience of many who have followed his teachings, that one can wake up here and now and shed the layers of ignorance which normally cloud one's view of the world. This awakening from the ordinary world in which we live is analogous to the waking up we each experience every morning when we arise from bed. It's a transition from experiencing the world in a dream state to seeing it more clearly. In Zen we take zazen as the foundation of this teaching, and this is why we place such emphasis on it in our practice.

"I said there is one man born in ancient India, the historical Buddha. He was born Siddhartha Gautama approximately 500 B.C.E. in northern India. He was the son of a king, and as with many religious figures, stories of a miraculous birth and of prophecy surround him. His father, the king, was told by a wise man that his son would become either a great king and leader of his people, or a religious leader. Preferring to continue the family business, the king raised his son in a highly protected environment, surrounded by beautiful young people and all of the pleasures the kingdom's wealth could provide. So when Siddhartha, in his twenties, left the palace overnight and saw a person suffering from sickness, he was horrified. 'What is this sickness?' he asked his attendant, but received no satisfactory answer. The young prince returned to the palace, but was to leave four more times. On his next two brief journeys he encountered first an old man and then a corpse carried on a bier, and unsuccessfully sought understanding from his attendant of old age and death. During his penultimate adventure he saw a mendicant of the kind then common in India. This was a person in shabby robes carrying a begging bowl and engaged in personal spiritual practice, and his attendant explained that this man was seeking the truth. Inspired, the following night Buddha scaled the palace walls and left for the forest, abandoning all that he had previously considered to be his life in order to undertake his own quest for the truth.

"Buddha practiced with all of the great spiritual teachers of his time, trying every path he could find, but none satisfied him, for none explained to him the true nature of the suffering of sickness, old age and death that he had seen. Eventually, despairing, he left to practice on his own and vowed to sit in

**131**

meditation until he either woke up to the truth or died trying.

"It was this very night that Buddha 'woke up,' and came back into the world, no longer Siddhartha Gautama, but Buddha, the Awakened One. He brought with him the simple teaching that captured his experience of the Four Noble Truths: the existence of suffering, the cause of suffering, the fact that it is possible to end suffering, and the path to do so, which he called the Noble Eightfold Path. The Four Noble Truths and the Noble Eightfold Path (right view, right thought, right speech, right action, right livelihood, right effort, right mindfulness, and right meditation) are the basis for all Buddhist teaching, and the massive libraries of texts are no more than editorials, commentaries, and expositions on them. It is not in intellectual understanding that these teachings reveal their wisdom, but in the practice of meditation. In fact, Buddha told his followers not to trust what he told them, but to find out the truth for themselves through meditation.

"Buddha gathered a great monastic and lay following during his life, which eventually included the wife, son, and mother he had left in the palace. When one of Buddha's followers demonstrated in his actions the same experiential insight of the truth that Buddha had enjoyed, the Buddha passed on to this individual, Mahakashyapa, his authority to teach. This transmission of authority from enlightened teacher to enlightened student became an important aspect of Buddhist practice, and to this day it is through Transmission that insight and wisdom are authenticated.

"Buddhism flourished in northern India for over 500 years, and branched north up the Silk Road, whence it went to Tibet and on into China, and south through Sri Lanka, to southern Asia. As it traveled, Buddhism retained its vitality and relevance by adapting the core practice of cultivating insight and awareness to the local customs, traditions, and religions of its new host countries. As a result Buddhist practice and culture is extraordinarily diverse, as diverse as all of the major religious traditions.

"The strand that left for China, which is known as the Mahayana or 'Great Vehicle,' gave rise to Zen. It flourished in China for almost a thousand years as Ch'an (a transliteration of the Sanskrit 'dhyana' for meditation), then migrated to Japan where, under the teacher Eihei Dogen (1200-1256), it became established as Soto Zen.

"Buddhism came to America with the waves of Asian immigrants in the nineteenth century, and strong practices were established in California. During the first part of the twentieth century, spiritual teachers from the East (famously including Vivekenanda, a Hindu) came to America to propagate their practices more widely, and by the middle of the century a small number of Buddhist teachers arriving from Japan founded their practice on teaching Westerners. One of these, Soyu Matsuoka Roshi, arrived from Japan in the 1930's, and beginning in Chicago, he founded the teaching practice that has given rise, though his transmitted student, Zenkai Taiun Michael Elliston (our Abbot), to the Atlanta Soto Zen Center.

"So here we are, practicing an American form of an ancient Indian practice. Any questions?"

Sophie and Simon both shake their heads.

"Okay, then let's talk about meditation."

## Zazen: Zen Buddhist Meditation

The presentation of meditation to newcomers is a very personal description of how to sit, in which the three areas of body/posture, breathing, and mind are addressed. It is personal both to the person providing the instruction, and to the visitors and their questions and responses, and it is because of this experiential aspect that I always encourage visitors to attend several newcomers' instructions given by different teachers, for they will get something different from each discussion.

All of the newcomers' meditation instructions come from the same simple place: the practice of zazen, the Zen form of meditation which is the primary focus of our practice. One of the most compact descriptions of this practice is offered by Dogen, our Japanese founder, in a treatise ("fukanzazengi") which he wrote for his monks:

> For practicing Zen a quiet room is suitable; eat and drink moderately
> Put aside all involvements and suspend all affairs
> Do not think "good" or "bad"; do not judge true or false
> Give up the operations of mind intellect and consciousness
> Stop measuring with thoughts ideas and views
> Have no designs on becoming a buddha
> How could that be limited to sitting or lying down?
> At your sitting place spread out a thick mat and put a cushion on it
> Sit either in the full-lotus or half-lotus position
> In the full-lotus position first place your right foot on your left thigh

then your left foot on your right thigh
In the half-lotus simply place your left foot on your right thigh
Tie your robes loosely and arrange them neatly
Then place your right hand on your left leg and your left hand on your
right palm
thumb-tips lightly touching
Straighten your body and sit upright leaning neither left nor right
neither forward nor backward
Align your ears with your shoulders and your nose with your navel
Rest the tip of your tongue against the front of the roof of your mouth
with teeth together and lips shut
Always keep your eyes open and breathe softly through your nose
Once you have adjusted your posture take a breath and exhale fully
rock your body right and left and settle into steady immovable sitting
Think of not-thinking not thinking what kind of thinking is that?
Nonthinking
This is the essential art of zazen.

These very simple instructions still form the foundation of our practice, though in modern America, many of us do not have the flexibility required to assume the full-lotus or half-lotus position. There are a variety of other postures which provide the stable tripod base that is the foundation for everything else Dogen describes, and to set the stage for not-thinking zazen. Nonthinking can be discussed at length, but its meaning is found in experience, not in intellectual discourse; it is not a cutting off of thoughts and emptying of the mind, but an acceptance of the mind as a thinking organ which excretes thoughts. In nonthinking we allow our thoughts to arise, abide, and decay, but we do not let ourselves get caught up in them; instead, we observe them without engaging them. We step back and let our mind think, but do not let the thoughts control us, dragging us involuntarily from one mental place to another.

I like to use examples to help people see why meditation must work; for Sophie and Simon I pick a favorite. "Think of a fly landing on your hand," I say. "Normally you'd just brush it off without even realizing it." Sophie and Simon nod. "Now imagine you've been sitting still for a while: this time, if the fly lands, you notice yourself brushing it off. If you've been sitting longer, maybe you notice your hand moving to brush it off; maybe later you notice the start of the movement; maybe still later you'll notice the impulse to move your hand before it actually moves. Does that make sense?"

Sophie and Simon nod again.

"Zazen uncovers all of our habit patterns just like this one. Once we shine the light of zazen on our lives, it's just a matter of time before the habits show themselves. And once they do, they can't ultimately survive as habits. We may choose to still do things—like brush away the fly—but it's volitional, not out of habit. And in the same way, as we engage in nonthinking, we look at our monkey mind, swinging from branch to disconnected branch, from thought to disconnected thought, anew. We begin to see the craziness of this logical, analytical mind of which we are so proud and see that in fact it is wildly erratic, and that we usually just let ourselves get dragged by it from thought to thought, immersed in all of the emotions and baggage that come with it. When we allow nonthinking to happen, we will gradually be able to sit to the side and watch the turbulent thoughts chasing around. It is refreshing not to be forced to follow them compulsively. So back to your concern, Sophie: zazen will indeed help your mind calm down."

Sophie nods, her original question answered.

"But a more peaceful mind is only a side effect of zazen, as are such things as sleeping better, getting sick less often, and feeling more useful. Zazen is first and foremost a spiritual practice, a journey deep into the self."

"You talked about the Four Noble Truths earlier," Simon says. "Zazen is obviously part of the path to end suffering, but you've not told us about the cause of suffering in the first place."

I nod and answer him. "Suffering is a translation of a Sanskrit word dukkha, which means 'discomfort,' 'dis-ease' (as in 'not at ease'), a sense of 'not fitting,' of 'something missing,' 'something wrong,' or 'something out of balance.' I understand the Chinese character for the word contains two wheels on an axle, one of which is off balance. It's awareness of this out-of-balance state, in some way shape or form, that usually brings folk to the spiritual path. And release from the condition comes from recognizing that we create this dukkha ourselves through our clinging mind that creates ideas and holds on to them—including, most perniciously, the self. Let me explain with an analogy:

*"If someone were to stick a knife in the back of my left hand, the right hand would come over to remove it without thinking 'I'm the right hand. The left hand is not me, so why should I bother to help? I've got better things to do,' and the like. The right hand would act intuitively out of a deep sense of connection with the left hand. In the same way each of us is connected to everything else,*

*both containing and contained within it, but we don't intuit this. Rather, we allow our sense of separate self-hood to get in the way: 'I'm the right hand, and these are my resources; I'll share some of them with the left hand because I'm a good person, but there's a limit!' "*

"It sounds like you're saying there's no soul," says Sophie.

"In Buddhism our experience—and it is an experience any legitimate teacher will tell you to go and verify or deny for yourself, not accept as doctrine—that this thing I call 'me' has no essence, nothing that is permanent."

"But isn't reincarnation something that's supposed to happen in Buddhism?" Sophie asks. "How can you have reincarnation if there's no soul?" I answer, "Actually we prefer to use the word 'rebirth' instead of 'reincarnation' for precisely that reason, but it's a complex idea, and like all ideas can really become a hindrance. 'What is it that is reborn?' is a great question that has been taken on by practitioners of Buddhism for years, and like all great questions the answers are experiential and found in practice, not by intellectual reflection. Sometimes it's best just to sit."

Sophie smiles. "You didn't really answer my question, but I guess that's something I'm going to have to get used to around here."

I smile back, put my palms together in front of my lower face, and make a small bow toward Sophie. I check that Simon is happy with the answer, ask if there are other questions, and then say, "We're going to go in and sit in the zendo in a minute, but first let me give you an overview of what to expect when you go in there."

## Zen Practices

Services at the Atlanta Soto Zen Center comprise mostly silent zen meditation, and they are open to all. We ask visitors to arrive five to ten minutes before the start of the service and introduce themselves to the attendant so that they can be shown 'the lay of the land,' but we are a very informal center and recognize the time constraints of our lives away from the center. Thus, we allow meditators to arrive and leave during the sitting period; all we ask is that people move slowly and quietly to minimize any distraction to others.

Individual sitting periods are typically twenty-five minutes long, and meditation periods comprise two or three such sessions separated by kinhin, or walking meditation. This is a practice of walking very slowly, roughly one half-step per breath, in a circle, and it both allows the stiffening of the legs that occurs in zazen to be relaxed, and provides a gentle move to integrate the mindfulness of zazen into everyday activity.

A large bell is sounded to end the sitting period and to indicate movement into the service. The meditators rise and face toward the center of the room.

The short service which follows commences when a senior teacher enters through the main door and offers incense at the altar. After the teacher has returned to the head of a mat which lies in front of the altar, chant cards are handed out. The form of the service differs slightly from time to time as we respect particular dates on the Buddhist calendar, but all of our services are anchored on the Heart of Great Perfect Wisdom Sutra (the "Heart Sutra" for short) and are actually quite simple. While it is possible to read the sutra with religious and philosophical intent, the intent of our service is that chants be offered without intellectual thought as an exercise in "just chanting" (analogous to the practice of "just sitting" in zazen) and in sharing community with the other attendees (called the sangha or "harmonious community").

The communal chants, including the Heart Sutra, are accompanied by one attendant (the "doan") marking the rhythm by hitting a large wooden drum of Japanese origin (called a mokugyo). This is carved in the shape of a fish with a large, hollowed- out head and a wide mouth, around which there are ornate carvings of dragons and pearls. (The symbolism is of a fire-breathing dragon returning to the water to put out the fire and quench its thirst.) The doan also strikes the various gongs occasionally at prescribed moments, each sounding having a certain function, whether to accompany an entrance or exit, to synchronize with the celebrant's (known as the "doshi") movements, or to indicate the timing for communal bows. These same gongs are struck to punctuate our meditation periods with short stretches of walking meditation (kinhin) and to indicate its end.

The service ends with announcements and an invitation for all to stay for the dharma talk (or, on weeknights, for whichever activity follows), which is generally a presentation by a teacher on a particular aspect of Buddhism, followed by a discussion in which all are asked to contribute their questions or comments. During the short break that separates the service from the talk, people stretch and scatter their cushions informally around the speaker's seat, while tea is brewed in the kitchen.

The dharma talk is delivered by one of the senior teachers, and while the particular personality and style of the talk will depend upon the individual, they are universally informal, with the intent of engaging the community in dialogue, and always leaving plenty of room for discussion and questions. On weeknights the form is more intentionally conversational, and the different teachers who lead each night (Monday through Thursday) each adopt a different format, generally focused on following a particular book or series of texts over several weeks.

In addition to the regular schedule of daily services, our Soto Zen Center offers a program of sesshin and zazenkai (longer and shorter zazen retreats). Sesshin, literally "to unify the mind," is an intensive meditation retreat offered periodically to deepen our practice. Characterized by extended introspection and silence, sesshin is a wonderful opportunity to receive personal guidance in private interviews with the teachers, to draw from the strength of the sangha practicing together, and to experience the deep stillness that lies within each one of us. During these retreats the primary activity is zazen, which is typically offered for eight or ten hours per day, and punctuated by excellent vegetarian food and one or two daily teachings.

Weekend or one-day zazenkai is offered every month at the in-town center, the first Saturday of the month. Longer sesshin retreats are offered periodically, generally at the in-town center, but occasionally at nearby retreat locations with overnight accommodations offering attendees the ability to completely immerse themselves in the practice. As a lay practice center, we rejoice in all participation that our members can arrange; still, we recognize that most have responsibilities which prevent full attendance, so many will attend portions of a sesshin or retreat.

### The Place of Worship and Its Symbolism

Once I've given visitors a brief overview of our practices, I lead them into the meditation hall.

Our zendo occupies a converted single-story office building in an old, light industrial district in metropolitan Atlanta. It is an old, unimposing building set in an area of surprising greenery, with a county parkland area beside it and Peachtree Creek a short walk through woodland to the rear. Entering through the main door, visitors find themselves in the first of a cluster of rooms of roughly equal size: to the right is the newcomers' room; straight ahead is the library, to one side of the library is a resident's room, and to the other a shower. Shoes are left on the shoe-rack in the library, and the zendo (or meditation hall) is accessed off a corridor that connects the two halves of our rented space (the other including our dining room and the kitchen).

Prior to entering the zendo, we stand just before the pine threshold and make a small bow with palms held together (a gesture known as "gassho") to indicate respect and mindfulness, then step through the doorway and between a pair of curtains into the room.

Our abbot, Zenkai Taiun Michael Elliston, spent his professional career as a designer and he, along with a number of the disciples including me, have invested considerable effort in making the space very special to us. The entrance to the thirty by thirty-foot square, carpeted room is in the middle of one of its four sides; the room is centered on four imposing pine-encased pillars which direct the visitor's attention directly ahead to the altar, while meditators sit facing the wall on a continuous bench that surrounds the room.

The benches are wooden with black fabric surfaces, on top of which three-foot-wide black padded mats sit in long rows. On top of each mat is a cushion, known as a zafu, or a seiza bench (for a kneeling zazen posture). The cushions and benches are of different sizes, and when I lead the visitors to their spaces on the bench, I ensure that they all have a zafu, a seiza bench, or an upright chair (yes, this is okay too!) with which they are comfortable. Later I will visit each, touch them in turn lightly on the left shoulder to indicate my presence, and make adjustments where necessary to their posture, to ensure they are erect, straight, and comfortable.

Sophie and Simon enter the hall in time to sit for a short while before kinhin, then sit for another period before the service. After the service I invite them to stay for the dharma talk and ask if they have any further questions. Sophie seems relaxed and plans to stay for the talk. Simon declares that he enjoyed the sit but is still curious. "Can you give me a quick tour? I'm interested in what all these statues and ornaments mean."

"Sure, we've got a few minutes before the talk, so let's start over here at the altar." I lead him to altar area and begin by pointing out, "You've probably noticed there are actually two altars. The smaller one at the front is used when the zendo is functioning as a meditation hall. When you first came in to meditate, the candle that you see on the back altar was right here, on this front altar. The larger altar at the back is used when we conduct our services, which is why we have not only the candle there, but also the incense burner for both the stick of incense and the chip incense we use during the service.

"The big altar has our 'big stuff': the large gold figure on top is the Buddha in seated meditation (the statue was brought from Japan by Matsuoka-

Roshi, our abbot's original teacher). It's important to note that Buddha is not a god, but rather a person we revere for 'waking up' without the need for a teacher, and a symbol for the Buddha-nature that we see in everything. When we prostrated before the statue, it was in reverence for the individual and for this Buddha-nature, and not the worship of a god."

"So what about all these other smaller statues scattered around?" Simon asks.

There are several: two small ones on the posts atop the altar, and three midsized statues on the altar itself. I gesture at them as I talk: "They have the same general meaning, but they also represent specific matters: pointing at the ground and the sky as a symbol for one of his teachings; palm raised with finger and thumb touching as a symbol for the act of teaching; and so forth. This one on the altar is of Avalokiteshvara (also known as Kannon in Japan and Guan yin in China), one of Buddha's original disciples who hears all of the sounds of suffering in the world."

"And these flowers?" Simon asks, pointing to two large vases with carved lotus flowers, one on each side of the altar.

"These were also brought to America by Matsuoka-Roshi, and until a couple of years ago they resided at a sister Zen Center in Chicago, where Matsuoka first taught and transmitted his teaching to our teacher and abbot. They show the lotus flower in its various stages, from young stem through bud to full flower, representing the brilliant flower of our ultimate awakening growing slowly from its origins in the deep, filthy muck at the bottom of a pond until it eventually emerges onto the surface of the water and opens fully."

"That's really interesting. You say Matsuoka 'transmitted' to your teacher. What does that mean?"

"That's the authority to teach, which we talked about earlier, as when Buddha saw his student Mahakashyapa had the developed insight and woke up. Matsuoka-Roshi saw this in his student and through a formal ceremony recognized Elliston-Roshi as his heir and the person to continue his lineage."

"The front altar looks pretty simple; is that golden image another statue of Buddha?" Simon waves his hand at the single statue.

"Actually that represents Manjushri, one of Buddha's original disciples. You see he's wielding a sword: symbolically that's to cut through illusion. And the stick at the front," I say, stepping round, bowing before picking up a three-foot long flat wooden rod, and holding it horizontally, bowing again and presenting it to the altar before letting it hang in my hands and showing it to Simon, "is called the kyosaku. That's actually the name of one of the texts containing Matsuoka-Roshi's teachings, and it is an item both he and Elliston-Roshi revere. It's used for posture correction, which is what you felt when someone came up behind you to straighten you while you were meditating; it's also used as a 'wake-up-stick.' Let me explain this. Sometimes, generally during longer retreats, people will raise their hands high and ask the attendant to use this to hit their shoulder. It works as a really deep massage, and it can provide great relief when you've been sitting for a long while. It can also literally help you wake up if you're getting drowsy.

"Now let's go over here." I lead him to the doan station, which is the place from which an attendant kept time and led the service. I'm about to start my description of the imposing array of gongs and the mokugyo when it becomes clear that folk are gathering for the service, so I keep it short. "In simple terms this is where the person who keeps the clock and runs the services sits. It's a position we rotate, and it requires a little training, but what matters for you is that we use drums and gongs to tell folk where we are in the service and what to do, and since these don't have the same emotional content as a voice, it helps with our practice. If you come here regularly, you'll start to recognize the symbols and follow them intuitively."

## Our Community

The Atlanta Soto Zen Center (ASZC) was founded in the early 1970's under the leadership of Abbot Zenkai Taiun Michael Elliston, who was a disciple of Rev. Dr. Soyu Matsuoka-Roshi in Chicago during the 1960's. Elliston-Roshi is the Zen Center's spiritual leader. We support our members by providing a sangha, or group to sit with, and experienced teachers who are available at all meditation sessions, as well as by email, phone, and appointment, to respond to any questions that arise.

Elliston-Roshi is a prolific teacher and writer, and is in regular attendance at the Atlanta Soto Zen Center. He also teaches regularly at local venues and visits affiliate centers elsewhere in the South and as far away as Wichita and Nova Scotia. Many of the abbot's teachings are available on the ASZC website, and those of his teacher, Matsuoka-Roshi, have been published in two volumes. We also have a natural affinity with the many Soto Zen centers throughout the U.S.

While we do not have a hierarchy as such, we do recognize that individuals pass through certain major steps as their practice evolves and they move into deeper levels of service to the sangha. The first step, jukai, is an initiation service in which persons essentially make a public statement about the importance of Buddhism to their lives, after which the community accepts them as members. A band to be worn around the neck (called a wagesa, which represents the border of Buddha's original robe) and a set of wrist beads (juzu beads, representing the one hundred and eight delusions which keep us from enlightenment, which become, when we stop to look at them, the one hundred and eight gates to our awakening) are given to each person during this service, and these are generally worn by the individual at the Zen Center. Initiates are encouraged to concentrate on their own personal practice for at least a year, and not to take on significant responsibilities at the Center. As they become more familiar and involved, their practice will naturally grow.

The growth of practice into deeper service will involve, for example, taking on organizational responsibilities, starting to manage the timekeeping and service operations as doan, and assisting with newcomers. This deepening commitment often will be recognized by an invitation to become a "disciple," and undergo a service known as ziake tokudo, during which the person is given a rakusu. This is a brown bib-like garment, worn on the chest, the front side of which is a patchwork square representing the Buddha's robe, and the back side of which is a certificate signed by the abbot. Disciples are encouraged to continue to deepen their personal practice, their sangha service, and to develop a stronger teacher-student relationship with the senior teachers and in particular with the abbot.

Some of our members have undergone a subsequent service known as "shukke tokudo" and become lay monks. These individuals are typically long-serving members who have developed a deep understanding of Buddhism and who serve in senior teaching positions. In anticipation of the service they sew a robe called an "okesa" which takes several months, and the sewing is itself a deeply contemplative practice.

Our primary community activities are oriented around meditation at the center, though they often include meals together. After the Sunday service we generally either have a potluck lunch (monthly) or a group of us will go out for lunch to a nearby Japanese/Thai restaurant. We occasionally have external activities and have also undertaken a program of quarterly activities within the Atlanta community, such as preparing food for the homeless and poor, and helping at a home for abused women.

## Zen and the Interfaith Dialogue

After the dharma talk I check in again with Sophie and Simon. Simon will be joining us as we go out for lunch, and I look forward to getting to know him better. Sophie has just one more question before she leaves to spend the afternoon on her academic activities. "I'm a Christian," she says. "Can I practice Zen and remain a Christian?"

This is a very good question which drives at something fundamental to our practice. "We talked earlier about whether Zen is a religion, a philosophy, or a lifestyle," I remind her, "and it certainly has all of these facets. Primarily, though, it is what you, personally, make of it that matters. The primary practice of Zen is zazen. This is profound, but at the same time it is a really simple, universal tool that is available to everyone. So from a Buddhist standpoint, you can come and practice with us and derive whatever benefit you like from our discussions and teachings, and remain a Christian. That's not the same thing, though, as saying you can be a Buddhist and a Christian, and I certainly can't speak to the view from the Christian side, which I suspect might be a little more difficult."

Sophie nods but asks for further explication.

"Buddhism is not a conversionistic practice and sees no conflict with other religions or practices. What we find, though, in our own experience, is that the practice of zazen helps all of us to settle down and to 'tune in' to that which connects us. We find zazen a very powerful tool in working with people who hold all kinds of belief systems, whether religiously oriented or otherwise. It is really interesting to compare a conversation among a group of people before they sit zazen together with that which occurs after they've sat.

"You might have noticed the sign outside the door that says, 'All who enter here are welcome; none who leave are pursued.' This phrase was first used by Sokei-An, a first-generation Buddhist teacher from Japan, at the Buddhist Society of America which he founded in New York City in the 1940s. It fits our practice perfectly.

"Buddhism does not hold for itself an exalted place, but rather, so long as the practice remains 'Buddhist,' it is recognized that this, too, is a labeling and categorization of that which is beyond. You heard me say earlier that when one hears the word 'Buddha' or 'Buddhism,' one should spit, and when one sees the Buddha on the road, one should kill him. These are obviously extreme ideas, but symbolically they mean that the practice of Buddhism should ultimately transcend

Buddhism itself. Is it true that so long as there are Jews, Christians, Muslims, Buddhists and Hindus, then there can be no genuine interfaith dialogue? Do not those very labels get in the way of authentic conversation? Or, is it possible that there is a place, a center, a Source from which all great religions draw that provides both a commonality and a richer experience of our particular faith? Perhaps Buddhism's place in interfaith dialogue is to provide a tool that leads us to a place beyond the labels where we can engage in the practice of, and conversation about, what truly matters."

# Glossary

**Avalokiteshvara** – The Sanskrit name for Kannon.

**Buddh** – The root Sanskrit word from which the Buddha's name is taken: it means to "wake up."

**Buddha** – The epithet given to Siddhartha Gautama after he "woke up" and returned to society to teach the spiritual path along which he had traveled. He became the founder of the tradition that has become known as "Buddhism." In Buddhism, though, it is accepted that many people wake up, and all are Buddhas (though the historical Buddha is held in a place of special reverence).

**Ch'an** – The Chinese name of the form of Buddhism that crossed to Japan and became Zen.

**Dharma** – A Sanskrit term for the teachings of Buddhism. It can also mean the elements of the world in which we live, which are themselves teachings.

**Dhyana** – A Sanskrit word for meditation. Transliterated into Chinese, it became "Ch'an," which was in turn transliterated into Japanese as "Zen."

**Dhukka** – A Sanskrit word generally translated into English as "suffering." The existence of dukkha and of the path to its cessation is the source from which Buddha drew his teachings, and the translation arguably does not do the word justice: it can be thought of as dis-ease, discomfort, a sense of something missing, something unstable, something out of balance or off-center.

**Doan** – The service attendant who: (a) keeps and signals (by means of bells, etc.) time during the periods of zazen; and (b) who accompanies the doshi in the service.

**Dogen** (1200-1256) – the founder of the Japanese strand of Buddhism known as "Soto Zen," which is the tradition that comes down to the Atlanta Soto Zen Center.

**Doshi** – The Zen teacher who leads the service.

**Four Noble Truths** – The original teaching of the Buddha: the existence of suffering, the cause of suffering, the fact that it is possible to end suffering, and the path to do so, which he called the Noble Eightfold Path. The Four Noble Truths and The Noble Eightfold Path are the basis for all Buddhist teaching.

**Fukenzazengi** – the first writing of Dogen on his return from Japan.

**Guan yin** – The Chinese name for Kannon.

**Jukai** – A ceremony of initiation into the Zen tradition.

**Juzu Beads** – Essentially a Buddhist rosary; the beads (in a multiple of twenty-seven) represent the one hundred and eight delusions which are our gateways for practice.

**Kannon** – An awakening being who hears all of the suffering in the world. This person is revered in most Buddhist traditions as a great example and teacher, and in addition to appearing on altars, his/her name is often used in chants.

**Kinhin** – A short period of walking meditation which separates two periods of zazen. The purpose is to allow the legs to relax, and to permit the experience of zazen to begin to penetrate into ordinary life.

**Kyosaku** – The three-foot stick that is used for posture correction in zazen, and for striking the shoulders of practitioners who actively ask for its use. Being struck by the kyosaku provides a deep massage and blows wandering thoughts out of the mind.

**Mahakashyapa** – A student of the historical Buddha whose "waking up" was recognized by Buddha when he transmitted to him the authority to continue his teachings.

**Mokugyo** – A large wooden drum shaped like a fish used by the doan in Zen services.

**Noble Eightfold Path** – The fourth of the Four Noble Truths taught by the Buddha, comprising right view, right thought, right speech, right action, right livelihood, right effort, right mindfulness, and right meditation.

**Okesa** – The robe worn by a Zen priest, symbolically representing the robe of the historical Buddha, and being a symbol of service as well as authority.

**Rakusu** – The "bib" worn by committed Zen practitioners who have undertaken Zaike Tokudo. It is a miniature representation of the Buddha's robe and is also a sign of service to the community, and a certificate of the Zaike Tokudo ceremony (marked on the back by the Abbot).

**Roshi** – An honorific title for a senior, transmitted Zen teacher

**Sangha** – The harmonious community. Generally this term refers to the community of Zen practitioners, but since Zen is all inclusive, it can be cast infinitely widely.

**Sesshin** – A period of intense practice, generally several days to a week long, with eight or ten hours of zazen each day.

**Seiza Bench** – A kneeling bench used for zazen.

**Shukke Tokudo** – The "home-leaving" ceremony undertaken by a Zen priest. In the tradition of ASZC, this home-leaving is both symbolic, and also represents "leaving home while staying at home," which means accepting broader responsibilities for and commitment to ASZC and the sangha.

**Wagesa** – A ribbon-like garment worn around the neck during zazen by initiates who have undertaken Jukai. It represents the border of Buddha's robe.

**Zabuton** – The three-foot mat on which a zafu or seiza bench is placed. It is used in zazen as a soft pad for the legs and knees.

**Zafu** – The round cushion used in zazen.

**Zaike Tokudo** – The ceremony of "discipleship" in which a Zen initiate takes on a greater commitment to the Zen path and a direct relationship as the student of Zen and of the Zen teacher conducting the service.

**Zazen** – The seated, objectless meditation practice which is central to Zen.

**Zazenkai** – A short period of intensive practice, generally a full day of eight or ten hours of zazen, book-ended by an evening and morning of zazen.

**Zen** – The lineage of Buddhism that arose in Japan and focuses on zazen as the center of practice.

**Zendo** – Both the building which ASZC operates, and the meditation hall within that building.

ଔ

## For Further Reading

*Dogen's Shobogenzo, translated by Nishijima and Cross.* Windbell Publications, 1996

*Flowers Fall by Hakuun Yasutani.* Shambhala Publications, 1996.

*Opening the Hand of Thought* by Kosho Uchiyama Roshi. Wisdom Publications, 2004.

*The Gateless Barrier* by Zenkei Shibayama. Shambhala Publications, 2000.

*The Kyosaku* by Matsuoka. Lulu, 2006.

*The Wholehearted Way* with commentary by Kosho Uchiyama Roshi, translated by Daniel Leighton. Tuttle Publishing, 1997.

*Zen Mind,* Beginner's Mind by Shunryu Suzuki. Weatherhill, 1973.

# Appendix I

## The Interfaith Immersion Weekend

The Interfaith Immersion Weekend offers people an opportunity to learn about other faiths through visiting their places of worship, sharing in conversations, and eating and praying together. It is more than information; it is an experience in which new relationships are born and new understandings emerge. Getting to know our religious neighbors is a high priority for today.

The description of the Sacred Spaces of the World's Five Major Religions, which you have read about in this volume, can become more than information by participating in an Interfaith Immersion Weekend.

Here is how one person evaluated the experience:

"When I returned from the Interfaith Immersion in Atlanta, I found myself sharing the experience with everyone who would listen. In particular, I spoke about community, about how each of the religions we experienced focused on creating and maintaining community in some form. Community provided strength, support, structure, and soul – all ingredients necessary for our walk with the Divine. Several of my fellow pilgrims touched my soul deeply through their friendship, insights, and guidance. I could not imagine anything greater that could happen to a person. What you have described is exactly what I hoped and prayed for would happen for the participants."

Increasingly we are living in a New World that involves the mixing of cultures and religions. This birth of a new age has been brought about by Internet technology, instant worldwide communication, and the ability to travel anywhere in the world within twenty-four hours. Cultures are encountering each other, and that means that in America we must understand and accept each other as equals before God.

For more information write to The InterFaith Community Institute,
669 East Side Street SE, Atlanta. GA 30316.
Phone: 404-906-7109.
Email: worldpilgrims@bellsouth.net
Webpage: http://www.interfaithci.org/

# SAMPLE SCHEDULE OF AN INTERFAITH WEEKEND

## Friday

9:00    Gathering & welcome at site convenient to participants. Introduction to the Weekend; introduction of the group; review of the schedule; orientation to the experience

10:00 -10:45    Presentation of Islam with discussion

11:00    Depart for restaurant near Masjid of Al-Islam

12:15    Lunch & orientation to Jumu'ah ( main Muslim Prayer Service)

1:00    Jumu'ah at Atlanta Masjid of Al-Islam

2:00    Conversation with Muslim friends

3:30    Depart for Al-Farooq Masjid (14th Street Mosque)

4:00    Tour and presentation at Al- Farooq Masjid

5:00    Personal prayer in the Masjid

5:30    Depart for home

## Saturday

8:00    Singing, introduction to Hinduism and Vedanta

9:00    Conversation with Presenter

10:30    Depart for Riverdale Hindu Temple

11:30    Tour of the Hindu Temple

12:15    Lunch with Temple participants at Riverdale

1:15    Depart for the Synagogue

2:00    What Jews believe about G-d, Torah/Jewish ethics, and community; (participants at tables, to facilitate group work) General interactive questions and answers, to include congregants. Discuss the elements in the sacred space.

2:30    Jewish meditation, chanting and mystical ways to experience G-d

3:30    Musical Sabbath afternoon/evening service, with Torah reading, ending with Havdallah (Sabbath ending service);

4:30    Thirty minutes to reflect on the day and the experience.

5:00    Depart for home

## Sunday

8:00    Coffee and fruit

8:30    Orientation to Buddhism

9:45    Depart for Buddhist Center

11:00    Share in the Buddhist meditation

12:15    Lunch together

1:30    Reflections on the Weekend

2:50    Closing Prayer

3:00    Depart

## Appendix 2

# *Meet Prophet Muhammad*
### *Builder of the First Mosque*

## Kemal Korucu and Mirkena Ozer

One night, over 1400 years ago...
In a city at the heart of a desert...
As the earth was cooling off from the heat of the day, something happened that would change the course of history. In a most unlikely place, in the Hira cave of the mountain Noor (light), a man sat in silence, pondering on his life and on his people. This man was a merchant by profession and was deemed trustworthy by character so that people called him Al Ameen (the trustworthy). He had reached middle age through a journey that had not yet come to its destination; on his retreat he was pondering the meaning of life and existence.

### A Prophet is born

He had never known his father, who died before his birth. His mother passed away when he was merely six years old. His grandfather Abdul Muttalib had sheltered this little orphan with great care and love. Later his uncle Abu Talib had seen that the child's needs were met till he reached youth. He had learned to trade but he disliked deceit. He had learned the tribal laws but he loathed injustice. He knew the idols that defiled the Kaaba, the sacred sanctuary, but he had never bowed before nor worshipped them. In his soul he had a longing for something different. He would seclude himself from this world where his soul suffered and find solace in the silent darkness of the Hira cave. His name was Muhammad, the praised one.

Little did Muhammad (peace be upon him – puh) suspect that the retreat on that night, which came to be known as the Night of Power, one of the many nights of Ramadan, the ninth month of the lunar year, would be like no other. Little did he know that from the darkness of that cave a light would spring forth and shine for centuries to come.

Unaware of the mission to which he would soon be called, Muhammad sat silently in the dark listening to his heart. All of a sudden he heard a most peculiar command to an unlettered man: "Read!"

True to his word Muhammad replied, "I don't know how to read."
The voice, unlike anything he had heard before, repeated: "Read!"

"I don't know how to read." He felt his heart beat fast and his body shake with a tremor. Who was asking of him something beyond his capacities? Right then Muhammad found himself in an embrace that almost took his breath away by its intensity. He thought he was going to die that very moment when verses started pouring from his mouth.

*Read! Read in the name of your Lord who created*
*Who created man from a clot*
*Read and your Lord is most gracious*
*He is who has taught by the pen*
*has taught man what he knew not.*

When the extraordinary embrace let go of him, Muhammad (puh) ran out of the cave and headed home in terror. What had happened just a moment ago? As he was climbing down the mountain, the mysterious voice that urged him to read inside the cave called him again: "I am Gabriel and you are the messenger of Allah."

Muhammad looked up and saw a being fill the horizon, a being so bright that Muhammad (puh) averted his eyes. Alas, everywhere he looked the angel was there repeating his message. "I am Gabriel and you are the messenger of Allah."

Muhammad knew Allah to be God, The Almighty in heaven, but what did it mean to be Allah's messenger?

### The Prophet finds support

Trembling convulsively, he hurried down the mountain. He passed the narrow streets of Mecca which looked eerie under the moonlight. His city was so quiet that the only sound he heard was his heart beating against his chest. Nothing seemed familiar anymore. He was shocked and couldn't speak. The only thing he could mutter to his wife Khadija as he dashed into the house was: cover me! Khadija, who loved him deeply, covered him with a blanket and waited patiently by his side till the tremor subsided. When he could speak again, he related the strange things that had happened to him.

"Khadija, I fear some evil spirit of the desert has gotten hold of me." Khadija smiled and caressed him. "You are the kindest person I know. You feed the poor and protect the weak. I don't think God would allow such a thing to happen to a good man like you. Wait, let me go to my cousin Waraqa. He has read the scriptures of Christians and Jews. He might know something."

Khadija ran fast to Waraqa and came back with an affirmation of the angel who had embraced him.

"Waraqa told me that the luminous being you saw is the archangel Gabriel. He has appeared to other prophets many times before. He brings messages from God to them. Waraqa thinks you have been chosen to be a messenger and what you experienced was the revelation. My love, the words you recited in the cave are the words of God." She ended her report with reverence toward Allah.

## The Message Spreads

On the days that followed, the revelations continued. God was telling the Prophet to call people to believe in one God and renounce the idols. He called people to be kind to one another, to tend to the needs of the poor and of orphans. This way of relating was something new for his people. Until then all they had known was the law of the tribe and clan, and if your clan was not wealthy or powerful your chances for prosperity and protection were grim. You could be wronged and no one would vindicate you.

The message Allah had given the Prophet was first spread in secret. The weak, the poor, the vulnerable gathered around him forming the first small circle of believers. Their hearts were touched by the eloquence of the verses revealed to Muhammad. These verses, which were collected and formed the Qur'an, were unlike any other verses they had ever heard, and they knew all about poetry. The Meccans took pride in two things more than others: their poetic skills and their trade. They entertained the merchants during annual fairs with their hospitality and fine poets, and that had paid off for them financially. Mecca was a prosperous trade center, one of the most important cities of the Arabian peninsula. But the Qur'an, with its unmatched beauty, was something else. Besides, Muhammad was no poet. He had not read or written anything before. He was unlettered.

## Persecution begins

One day the Prophet was ordered by God to proclaim his message openly to all people. That was the day when the hardships and persecutions began to be unleashed, threatening the new community with extinction. For more than a decade the persecution continued, culminating in the expulsion of the first Muslim community from Mecca. During those years insults, tortures, attempts at assassination were aimed at Muhammad (puh).Yet he stood fast in the face of this hostility and continued his mission. He continued calling people to God, to virtue, to justice and kindness.

In the search for asylum Muhammad sent a group of believers, those with no clan protection, to Abyssinia where a just Christian king ruled. King Negus proved the prophet right by providing refuge to the believers fleeing from persecution.

At one point the Muslim community in Mecca underwent a strict two-year boycott. The powerful chieftains of Mecca declared that either Muhammad (puh) and his followers would give up their new religion and return to the idols or they would die of starvation in isolation. No Meccan would trade with them or even speak with them. Those two years were the hardest for the Prophet and his followers because with all ties cut, survival became a serious struggle. A community of men, women, children and seniors were abandoned to death because they renounced the idols and believed in One God.

When, by a miracle, the boycott was lifted, hostility towards Muslims still continued. Muhammad's uncle and his main protector, Abu Talib, died. In the same year his beloved wife Khadija also left this world of hardship for her eternal abode. Again the Prophet felt orphaned. This year in Islamic history is labeled as the year of sorrow. The verses revealed at this time provided solace for the Prophet's soul. Other prophets also had endured oppression, ridicule, persecution; why would it be different with Muhammad? Yet despite the persecutions, the triumph belonged to him and the believers because they were on God's side. The Almighty was his helper and his protector.

### In Search of Safety

With faith and hope Muhammad started to look for neighboring cities where he and his community could take refuge. He visited Taif, but the people of this city called him a majnun, a madman, and drove him away, inciting the children to throw stones at him.

Meanwhile the chieftains of Mecca were plotting to kill Muhammad (puh) and to extinguish the flame of this new religion once and for all. It looked as if the small group of believers had no way out. Yet, it is in the darkest hour

154

of the night when the dawn draws closer.

Indeed that very thing happened. A group of people from Yathrib, a city built on an oasis north of Mecca, came to him and invited the Prophet to their city to be an arbiter because tribes in that city were always warring with each other. This city was home to two main tribes that were hostile to each other and were frequently caught up in squabbles. These two were the Haws and the Khazraj. Also living in the city were three Jewish tribes who operated the market and owned date palm plantations. The group of people from Yathrib who called on the Prophet promised to protect him and his followers with their own lives if necessary.

## Move to Medina

The Prophet agreed to go. So he and all his followers left their homes and immigrated to Yathrib, which later came to be called Medina. They had to leave Mecca in secret and in pain. Those who have experienced exile know how hard is to leave everything behind and move toward the unknown on an unbidden path.

When they arrived, the Prophet and the believers were warmly welcomed in Medina. The Prophet laid out regulations that guaranteed the rights of all inhabitants to property, protection, and freedom of religious practices. This pact, known as the Constitution of Medina, was accepted by all the tribes living there: the Muslims, the Jews and the polytheists.

## The first Mosque

In his early days in Medina, the Prophet decided to built a masjid, a place of worship for Muslims. This was a thrilling experience. They were free not only to practice their religion, but also to build a public place for that purpose. When the plot of land was purchased and the construction begun, the whole community wanted to be part of this unique endeavor. Some carried mud bricks, some made them. Some carried water to soften the hard earth, others dug into its bosom to lay the foundation of the place where they would worship God without fear. On that day the Prophet himself worked harder than anybody else. Defying his fifty-three years of age, he was an example of a work ethic worthy of others to follow.

As we look back in time, as we recall those people who worked diligently under the sun, we wonder if this first community of Muslims realized that they were laying a foundation for something far greater than just a building? Could they have believed that years later Islam would stop being a religion of a minority and that many other masajid (the plural of masjid) would be erected all over Arabia? Could they have imagined as they laid mud bricks, one on the top of the other, that one day masajid would become admirable architectural masterpieces in capitals of the world such as Baghdad, Istanbul, , Cordoba and Granada? Would they have believed at that time that the roof of the masjid they were covering with palm tree branches would be replaced by awe-inspiring domes, inlaid with gold or silver shimmering under the sun, a sacred place visited by millions of people every year?

Probably not. And it is less likely that they could imagine a land undiscovered, a land to be named America after the explorer who set foot on it, a land where diverse religious communities thrive due to its tolerant, rich spiritual soil. But it is true. It came to be. Islam has made the journey and now it is part of America. So it is not a surprise to encounter Muslims, entering with reverence a place they cherish and love. And they call it a masjid.

 CR

## About the authors

**Kemal Korucu**. Born in Turkey, Kemal came to the U.S. in 1986 to study computer science at Georgia State University. He owns two businesses – a software company and a Turkish grocery store – and has been happily married to Meral since 1998. He says, "As individuals we may feel powerless, even depressed, about the world. What it needs is for people of faith to join together to solve our common problems. We start by getting to know each other."

**Mirkena Ozer** graduated from Tirana State University, with a major in Turkish and Balcanic Studies and is currently pursuing a Masters in Women's Studies at Georgia State University. She is married with four children and gives talks on Islam, Culture, and Women's Issues.

Made in the USA
Middletown, DE
16 March 2015